EYE ON
Art

POTTERY

by Phyllis Raybin Emert

LUCENT BOOKS
A part of Gale, Cengage Learning

37268000137596

GALE
CENGAGE Learning™

Detroit • New York • San Francisco • New Haven, Conn • Waterville, Maine • London

LIBRARY OF CONGRESS CATALOGING-IN-PUBLICATION DATA

Emert, Phyllis Raybin.
  Pottery / by Phyllis Raybin Emert.
     p. cm. — (Eye on art)
  Includes bibliographical references and index.
  ISBN 978-1-4205-0046-2 (hardcover)
  1. Pottery—Juvenile literature. I. Title.
  NK4240.E44 2009
  738—dc22
                                                    2008040894

Lucent Books
27500 Drake Rd.
Farmington Hills, MI 48331

ISBN-13: 978-1-4205-0046-2
ISBN-10: 1-4205-0046-5

Printed in the United States of America
1 2 3 4 5 6 7 12 11 10 09 08

CONTENTS

Thank you to Silvestra Puente Praino and Delores Bostrom, reference librarians, Mahwah Public Library, Mahwah, New Jersey, without whose help this book would not have been possible. Special thanks to Larry Emert and clay artist Twyla Wardell.

Foreword

"Art has no other purpose than to brush aside . . . everything that veils reality from us in order to bring us face to face with reality itself."

—French philosopher Henri-Louis Bergson

Some thirty-one thousand years ago, early humans painted strikingly sophisticated images of horses, bison, rhinoceroses, bears, and other animals on the walls of a cave in southern France. The meaning of these elaborate pictures is unknown, although some experts speculate that they held ceremonial significance. Regardless of their intended purpose, the Chauvet-Pont-d'Arc cave paintings represent some of the first known expressions of the artistic impulse.

From the Paleolithic era to the present day, human beings have continued to create works of visual art. Artists have developed painting, drawing, sculpture, engraving, and many other techniques to produce visual representations of landscapes, the human form, religious and historical events, and countless other subjects. The artistic impulse also finds expression in glass, jewelry, and new forms inspired by new technology. Indeed, judging by humanity's prolific artistic output throughout history, one must conclude that the compulsion to produce art is an inherent aspect of being human, and the results are among humanity's greatest cultural achievements: masterpieces such as the architectural marvels of ancient Greece, Michelangelo's perfectly rendered statue *David*, Vincent van Gogh's visionary painting *Starry Night*, and endless other treasures.

The creative impulse serves many purposes for society. At its most basic level, art is a form of entertainment or the means for a satisfying or pleasant aesthetic experience. But art's true power lies not in its potential to entertain and delight but in its ability to enlighten, to reveal the truth, and by doing so to uplift the human spirit and transform the human race.

One of the primary functions of art has been to serve religion. For most of Western history, for example, artists were paid by the church to produce works with religious themes and subjects. Art was thus a tool to help human beings transcend mundane, secular reality and achieve spiritual enlightenment. One of the best-known, and largest-scale, examples of Christian religious art is the Sistine Chapel in the Vatican in Rome. In 1508 Pope Julius II commissioned Italian Renaissance artist Michelangelo to paint the chapel's vaulted ceiling, an area of 640 square yards (535 sq. m). Michelangelo spent four years on scaffolding, his neck craned, creating a panoramic fresco of some three hundred human figures. His paintings depict Old Testament prophets and heroes, sibyls of Greek mythology, and nine scenes from the Book of Genesis, including the Creation of Adam, the Fall of Adam and Eve from the Garden of Eden, and the Flood. The ceiling of the Sistine Chapel is considered one of the greatest works of Western art and has inspired the awe of countless Christian pilgrims and other religious seekers. As eighteenth-century German poet and author Johann Wolfgang von Goethe wrote, "Until you have seen this Sistine Chapel, you can have no adequate conception of what man is capable of."

In addition to inspiring religious fervor, art can serve as a force for social change. Artists are among the visionaries of any culture. As such, they often perceive injustice and wrongdoing and confront others by reflecting what they see in their work. One classic example of art as social commentary was created in May 1937, during the brutal Spanish civil war. On May 1 Spanish artist Pablo Picasso learned of the recent attack on the small Basque village of Guernica by German airplanes allied with fascist forces led by Francisco Franco. The German pilots had used the village for target practice, a three-hour bombing that killed sixteen hundred civilians. Picasso, living in Paris, channeled his outrage over the massacre into his painting *Guernica*, a black, white, and gray mural that depicts dismembered animals and fractured human figures whose faces are contorted in agonized expressions. Initially, critics and the public condemned the painting as an incoherent hodgepodge, but the work soon came to be seen as a powerful antiwar statement and remains an iconic symbol of the violence and terror that dominated world events during the remainder of the twentieth century.

The impulse to create art—whether painting animals with crude pigments on a cave wall, sculpting a human form from marble, or commemorating human tragedy in a mural—thus serves many purposes. It offers an entertaining diversion, nourishes the imagination and the spirit, decorates and beautifies the world, and chronicles the age. But underlying all these functions is the desire to reveal that which is obscure—to illuminate, clarify, and perhaps ennoble. As Picasso himself stated, "The purpose of art is washing the dust of daily life off our souls."

The Eye on Art series is intended to assist readers in understanding the various roles of art in society. Each volume offers an in-depth exploration of a major artistic movement, medium, figure, or profession. All books in the series are beautifully illustrated with full-color photographs and diagrams. Riveting narrative, clear technical explanation, informative sidebars, fully documented quotes, a bibliography, and a thorough index all provide excellent starting points for research and discussion. With these features, the Eye on Art series is a useful introduction to the world of art—a world that can offer both insight and inspiration.

The Origins
of Pottery

The beginnings of pottery may be a consequence of numerous lines of experimentation and accumulation of practical experience.
—Prudence M. Rice, *Pottery Analysis*

It is easy to imagine primitive people grabbing a lump of clay near a river or lake and forming it into human or animal shapes, and then finding that as the clay dried, it hardened. Clay animal and fertility figures found at a site in the Czech Republic estimated to be around thirty thousand years old are the earliest discovered pottery. Clay sculptures of bison discovered in Tuc d'Audobert Cave in France are thought to be about fourteen thousand years old.

Many theories explain the transition from simple clay figures to actual functional vessels. At first, ancient people made containers from materials found around them, including animal skins and bladders, wood, stone, and baskets they wove together from coarse grasses or plants. They also used clay to line fire and storage pits and to reinforce their baskets to make them waterproof.

A basket might have been left too long near the fire, and perhaps someone observed that the hotter the clay became, the harder and less porous it got. The next logical step would have been to create fired vessels of clay that could be used for cooking and for storage. "It is not difficult to imagine that once people recognized the durability and impermeability of the hardened clay . . . ," wrote ceramic analyst and professor Prudence M. Rice, "they would have experimented with firing clay to create portable containers."[1]

Depending on the availability of food and water, some early societies were nomadic, meaning that they moved from one place to another. If resources were plentiful, people lived together in one general area. They hunted, may have kept animals, and farmed the land. These are called sedentary societies. Both groups made and used pottery, but the sedentary groups played a more important role in improving pottery and finding more uses for it.

Editors William K. Barnett and John W. Hoopes state, "It is a mistake . . . to infer the existence of either sedentism or agriculture from the presence of pottery alone. . . . [But] there is no doubt that sedentism, even when seasonal, played a significant, positive role in the emergence of ceramic technology."[2] Staying

These sculptures of clay bison from the Tuc d'Audobert Cave in Saint-Germain-en-Laye, France, are thought to be about fourteen thousand years old.

in one place allowed for a permanent production site, which resulted in better production methods and higher-quality vessels for different uses.

Supply and demand also had a role in improving the quality of pottery vessels. People needed nonporous, fire-resistant containers in which to cook seeds and grains such as rice, wheat, or maize to make them edible. This required boiling in a pot that could be left on the fire for long periods of time without burning or breaking apart. Specialized pottery vessels were made to cook meats, vegetables, and fish. As the array of foods increased, so did the variety of pots used to cook and store them.

Pottery Making, the Role of Women, and Community Feasts

In most societies, women were in charge of the household. Women were usually responsible for tasks such as cooking, so they had an interest in creating better tools for this work. One theory, according to some archeologists, holds that pottery making was the first "woman's technology."[3] It allowed females, who selected the grains, then processed and cooked them, the time for other household tasks.

According to archaeologist D.E. Arnold, the role of women in pottery making fit in well with raising children and managing the household. Women did not have to leave home to make pottery. It was safe and did not require their complete attention. They could still focus on other domestic chores like cooking, cleaning, and child care. [4]

Other theories about the development of pottery focus on the importance of feasts among ancient people. Community banquets brought about increased production of pottery pieces, which were used only for these particular occasions. When others were invited to the festivities, a large display of pottery and food were examples of the wealth and power of the community and its generosity.

Clues to the Past

The collection and study of pottery fragments called shards provide clues about the daily lives and beliefs of ancient cul-

tures and the development of early societies. Pottery is a reflection of the people who made it. The materials used in making pottery, production methods, ornamentation, and decoration help to reveal the history, social behavior, and attitudes of the society that manufactured it.

Thus, the collection and study of pottery artifacts provide priceless information about ancient cultures. It is especially important to know the age of the pottery pieces. Archaeologists use several methods to determine the age of artifacts.

Dating Pottery

Absolute (or chronometric) dating determines the approximate year the pottery was made. The three types of absolute dating methods are radiocarbon, archaeomagnetism, and thermoluminescence.

Radiocarbon dating is based on the radioactive decay of the isotope carbon 14, which is contained in all living things. Since pottery has never been alive, this method cannot be used accurately. Rice writes, it "has . . . been applied experimentally to pottery containing 1% or more organic matter,"[5] if, for example, animal waste or plant pieces were included in the original clay mixture.

Archaeomagnetic dating measures the magnetism of certain minerals that are present in clay. Rice notes that this method is used to date kilns "or other burned areas associated with ancient firing."[6] In thermoluminescence dating, the pottery is heated in a laboratory to 932°F (500°C). According to Rice, "The amount of light emitted in this reheating . . . will be proportional to the age of the piece since its last heating (presumably its original firing)."[7]

Relative dating determines only whether the object is older, younger, or similar in age to other objects. There are two types of relative dating. Cross dating is based on similar styles of pottery found at different locations and thus assumed to be of the same time period. Sequence dating deals with the arrangement of objects in an order based on similarities in decoration or other characteristics.

Pottery Basics

Pottery was the first synthetic material humans created . . . and it combines the four basic elements identified by the Greeks: earth, water, fire, and air. As one of many materials within the large sphere of technology known as ceramics, pottery has transformed a broad range of human endeavors, from prehistoric cuisine to the twentieth-century aerospace industry.

—Prudence M. Rice, *Pottery Analysis*

Pottery is a general term used for any fired piece of clay, but there are different kinds of clay and various types of pottery, from terra-cotta and earthenware to stoneware and porcelain. Pottery making involves clay preparation, building techniques such as hand-formed and wheel-thrown methods, the decoration process, and then firing the clay in kilns.

The terms *pottery* and *ceramics* can be used interchangeably, especially when talking about functional and artistic pieces made from fired clay. However, while pottery deals exclusively with objects made from clay, the advanced ceramics field also includes technological advances such as tiles for the space shuttle, fiber-optics communications, and cellular phones, among many other categories.

Ingredients and Types of Clay

Clay is a natural material formed from the decomposition of rocks. When mixed with water, it has plasticity, which means that it can be molded and will hold a shape. Clay is mostly hydrated silicate of aluminum and will harden when dry, but if soaked in water, it will become clay once more. The application of heat transforms clay into pottery. This process is called firing. Once clay is fired, it will never be clay again.

According to Rice, "By the late Paleolithic period [about 40,000 to 10,000 B.C.] three significant principles of clay use were already known. One is that moist clay is plastic. . . . Another principle is that fire hardens clay. A third is that adding various substances to clay can improve its properties and usefulness."[8]

Different kinds of clay make different types of pottery. Clay may vary with regard to color, coarseness, and impurities. Some clays will shrink or warp during firing, while others stand up to intense heat.

The purest form of clay and the most prized is called kaolin or china clay, which is an important ingredient (along with feldspar and quartz) in making the finest porcelain. Porcelain is desired for its purity and whiteness. Although it is not completely transparent, light can pass through it. Porcelain has a nearly zero percent porosity, which means it does not absorb water, and it makes a clear musical ring when tapped. Deposits of kaolin are found in the southeastern part of the United States, England, and Germany. In Asia these clays are found in China, Japan, and Korea.

Ball clays are similar to kaolin. They are highly plastic, easily shaped, and fine-grained. When fired, ball clays are off-white to cream colored. Deposits are found in England as well as Kentucky and Tennessee in the United States. Another type of clay, found in abundance throughout the world, is fire clay. Fire clays range in color from tan to red to dark brown. This strong, coarse clay is used to make bricks, drain pipes, and other heavy-duty products.

Clay Preparation: Aging and Wedging

Clay is carefully prepared before beginning the process of shaping it into a vessel. Potters still use many of the same ancient

RITUALS AND RULES IN OBTAINING CLAY

In some societies, according to tradition, not just anyone can gather clay or make pottery. Ceramic analyst and professor Prudence M. Rice describes the requirements for obtaining clay in Papua New Guinea:

*A*mong the Azera of Morobe Province . . . only married women who have not yet had children can gather clay, and then only at certain times. They must wear traditional dress while gathering clay, and they cannot smoke. . . . In addition, outsiders are forbidden to witness the activity. . . . Among the Sepik River Kwoma . . . pots may be made only by married women who have borne two or three children. . . . Washing, loud conversation, wood chopping . . . and digging yams . . . are all forbidden during Kwoma pottery making.

Prudence M. Rice, *Pottery Analysis*. Chicago: University of Chicago Press, 1987, pp. 115, 124.

methods used by early potters. Clay used to make pottery must have plasticity to be suitable for shaping and molding. Aging the clay for weeks or even months is recommended. Clay can be stored in heavy-duty plastic bags or closed containers in a cool, dry place for long periods of time. The clay must be kept moist at all times and away from any heat source. A small amount of water can be added and mixed in if the clay dries or hardens.

A process called wedging is necessary before shaping the clay. Air pockets and bubbles can cause a vessel to crack or break during firing. The clay should be twisted, banged, and kneaded out with the heel of the hand to remove the air bubbles. Some potters add additional material to the clay at this stage. They add finely crushed shells, sand, and even fiberglass for strength and to prevent sagging.

Shaping Clay: Pinching and Coiling

Several methods can be used to shape pottery by hand, and sometimes more than one technique is used in the creation of a single piece. "Hand-building with clay is one of the oldest craft activities known," write authors Glenn C. Nelson and Richard Burkett. "Potters use . . . [hand-building] techniques in almost the same manner as they were used 10,000 or 12,000 years ago."[9] Pinching is a technique that shapes the clay, usually from a single ball, by working it between moistened fingers and thumbs. Pinch pots are simple vessels made by using the thumb to indent the center and rotate deeper until the sides and bottom are shaped into a bowl. Pressure applied evenly to the clay

HOW POTTERY MAKING CAME TO THE KALINGA

Archaeologist William A. Longacre wrote about the origin of pottery making as told to him by a person named Lingayo in the Dangtalan area of the Philippines in 1975. Lingayo related:

People here in the mountains originally came from the lowlands. Ever since, they have called their god Kabunyan. During those early days Kabunyan was traveling in the mountains with his son. . . . He went down to Dangtalan and there he looked for a container so he could cook his rice. Because he could not find a pot, he made one out of clay that he dug up right at Dangtalan. He cooked his rice and that evening he left his pot where he had cooked. So the people saw the pot made by Kabunyan and they also knew how he had made it because they had watched him. The people now knew how to make pots and that is why the women of Dangtalan are potters today.

Quoted in William K. Barnett and John W. Hoopes, *The Emergence of Pottery*. Washington, DC: Smithsonian Institution Press, 1995, p. 277.

stretches it and smoothes over any cracks. Then various textures can be applied to the surface

One of the oldest pottery-making techniques is coil building. This involves rolling the clay into coils or ropes, then building up the walls of a vessel by placing one coil on top of another on a clay base until the desired height is reached. The coils can be pressed and smoothed together with water. Ancient cultures made many large, thick-coiled pots and used wet paddles to thin and shape the walls of the vessel. The coil-building method was also used in large sculptural works. Other handmade pottery methods include clay molds and slab construction.

Molds and Slabs

Since ancient times, molds have been used to produce pottery with speed and efficiency and only minor variations from one piece to another. The molds are made from plaster, wood, or other materials. Pots, bowls, and other functional vessels are often made from molds.

"Artists use molds as a starting point for even more complex forms,"[10] declare authors Nelson and Burkett. The clay is pressed into the mold to assume the shape and is removed after partial drying. Powdered clay or ash help to prevent the clay from sticking to the mold.

Slab building is another ancient method of shaping clay by hand. Clay slabs of varying thicknesses and sizes are joined together to produce pottery shapes. Slab building is often used to create very large vessels in rectangular and cylindrical shapes and also for pieces such as platters and heavy bowls.

Development of the Potter's Wheel

When a clay vessel is created by hand, it is necessary to turn the piece around to shape and smooth it. Historian and potter Emmanuel Cooper writes, "Most of the early potters sat on the floor and probably used either the inside of their thighs to support the pot or rested it on a disc or mat on the floor in front of them. This enabled the pot to be turned round much more

In Gunupur, India, a village potter throws pots on a kick wheel. The advantage of making pots on the wheel is that you can make perfectly rounded forms in a short period of time.

easily."[11] The development and evolution of the potter's wheel changed the face of pottery production in the Old World.

Historians disagree about when the first potter's wheel was used. Rice states it was commonly used by the Middle Bronze Age, after 2250 B.C. Historians Cooper and Robert J. Charleston note wheel use in Mesopotamia about 3500 B.C., while artist and educator Susan Peterson declares that "use of the potter's wheel dates from about 5000 B.C. beginning in Egypt, the Middle East, and Asia."[12]

Although the date of origin may not be exact, the potter's wheel developed from a simple form that rested on the ground and was turned on a shaft or pivot by hand or with a stick. This evolved into a design where the potter could sit and turn the wheel. There are two basic types of wheels, the stick wheel and the kick wheel. Rice explains "The stick wheel . . . has a large head and a short axle . . . the head itself has sufficient weight to maintain the momentum . . . [and] . . . is rotated by inserting a stick into a hole in the top and turning it thirty or forty revolutions. This is enough to cause the apparatus to spin on its own for as much as five minutes without stopping."[13]

Rice states that "the kick wheel consists of a wheel head and a flywheel joined by a vertical axle."[14] The potter sits and works the clay on the upper wheel while simultaneously kicking the lower wheel, which provides the energy to rotate the upper wheel. The faster the potter kicks the lower wheel, the faster the upper wheel will rotate.

Peterson and her husband built one of the first motorized potter's wheels in 1950 with a foot pedal that controlled the speed of the wheel, though many potters continue to use traditional hand or kick wheels. "The overriding advantage of the wheel is that one can make perfectly symmetrical rounded forms in a short time,"[15] write Nelson and Burkett. Working pottery directly on the wheel is called "throwing the clay."

Throwing the Clay and Decorating the Surface

To throw clay, the potter places a mound of clay on the rotating wheel and forms it into shape with the fingers and hands. The clay is sensitive to squeezing, pressure, and the speed of the wheel. It takes many hours of practice to learn to use a pottery wheel well enough to turn a lump of clay into a well-formed piece of pottery. Various tools are used to smooth, decrease, trim, cut, and perfect the finished form, including sponges (with water), cut-off wires, and a potter's knife. Handles, bases, lids, rims, and spouts can be added to the form while the clay is still soft and malleable.

Once the piece has its shape, the potter can apply various finishes to decorate the surface. Burnishing makes it smoother, shinier, stronger, and more waterproof. This is done using a flat, hard stone, a cloth, or different tools to polish the surface before firing. Oftentimes, clay and water are mixed together to make another type of finish called a slip, which is applied to the surface of the pottery to make it stronger and less porous. Potters often use colored slips and paints as decoration. Pottery textures are varied by carving lines (incising) and other designs or pressing basket or weave patterns (stamping) into the surface.

Pouring or squeezing slip onto a smooth surface creates patterns and raised lines on the pottery. This process is called slip trailing. Englobe, similar to slip, is liquid or gel-like clay mixed with metallic oxides and other materials that create various colors on the surface. The pottery may also be covered in glaze. Glaze is made from silica, which forms a glassy layer; a flux, such as lead, alkaline, and boron compounds, which lower the melting point and combine with the silica; and a refractory ingredient like alumina that makes it harder and stronger. When fired, glaze applied to pottery creates a glasslike coating on the surface.

Early cultures experimented with different combinations of metals, minerals, and other substances in glazes to determine what color resulted and whether the color changed during firing at various temperature levels.

Kiln Development

The firing process turns the clay into a permanent piece of pottery. This process evolved from an open fire to a pit and then to an enclosed area like a cave, where a hotter fire produced stronger and harder pottery. Like the potter's wheel for shaping the clay, the development of kilns for firing clay pots changed the face of pottery. The first kilns were enclosed chambers that collected and controlled the heat from a wood fire. Today, different types of kilns are fueled by wood, coal, oil, gas, or electricity, but the basic process is the same. Artist and educator Dora M. Billington

The pottery shown in the foreground was created by using the furnaces pictured in the background. It is the firing that makes clay into a piece of permanent pottery.

The amount of oxygen within the kiln will determine the color of the pottery being fired. A reduction (or reducing) atmosphere in which the oxygen is limited may be smoky from excess carbon, as compared to a clean oxidation (or oxidizing) atmosphere. These kiln conditions will especially affect pottery that contains iron and copper oxides. "In reduction glazes," writes ceramicist Peter Lane, "iron can give colours ranging from delicate greens, blues and greys through deep olive to rust-red and black according to the proportions used. The usual greens and blues produced from copper oxides in glazes fired under clean, oxidizing conditions are transformed into an amazing variety of pinks, reds, and purples in the reduction kiln."

A raku-fired pot being fired in a kiln. The amount of oxygen in the kiln determines the color of the finished pot.

Peter Lane, *Studio Ceramics*. Radnor, PA: Chilton, 1983, p. 222.

describes a firing: "The pots are placed in the kiln while it is still cold, then heat is applied gradually and evenly to the maximum necessary, maintained for a while . . . and then just as gradually and evenly cooled down again; and the pots are not taken out until they are cool enough to handle freely."[16]

Clay that has been fired into pottery is divided into two categories, depending upon the temperature in the kiln. These categories are vitrified or nonvitrified pottery. If the kiln temperature is high enough to cause a process in which the clay melts and changes into a glassy material, the result is vitrified pottery. This process does not occur in nonvitrified pottery. The higher the kiln temperature, the harder and more waterproof the pottery will be. Traditionally, fired pottery pieces are divided into three broad types: earthenware, stoneware, and porcelain.

Earthenware: Low-Fired Non-vitrified Pottery

Earthenware is nonvitrified and often fired at a range of temperatures up to 2,192°F (1,200°C). Earthenware can be either unglazed or glazed, and usually fired to a reddish brown color, caused by the high content of iron oxide in the earthenware clays used. Peterson describes earthenware as "relatively soft, chalky, porous, breaks easily, leaks liquids, is not acid or stain resistant, and is light in weight. . . . On the other hand, earthenware pieces have some thermal shock resistance due to their porosity, making them useful for certain cookware and outdoor sculpture in hot-and-cold climates."[17]

Terra-cotta pottery is often categorized as earthenware, but some scholars list terra-cottas as a separate type. According to Rice, "Terra-cottas are relatively coarse, porous wares fired at low temperatures, usually 1,652°F (900°C) or less. The earliest fired pottery in all areas of the world falls into this category."[18]

Although some scholars list terra-cottas, like this Paleolithic era two-handled jug (3000–2700 B.C.) as a separate type of pottery, terra-cotta is often categorized as earthenware.

Terra-cottas are often unglazed but may be covered with an outer mixture of clay and water, which decorate the vessel as well as help stop liquid from leaking out.

Clay pots being fired on a wood fire by a Somali potter. A hotter fire results in a different type of pottery.

Stoneware and Porcelain: High-Fired Vitrified Pottery

Stoneware is fired at a higher temperature than earthenware, from 2,192°F to 2,462°F (1,200°C to 1,350°C). The hotter firing results in a finished product that is stronger, harder, and less porous than earthenware. Stoneware ranges from a light tan to dark brown in color with coarse textures and can be lead- or salt-glazed.

"The pinnacle of the potter's art, at least in terms of technical accomplishments, was reached with the Chinese production of porcelain,"[19] declares Rice. This highly prized, pure white, vitrified pottery is fired at a temperature range of 2,336°F to 2,552°F (1,280°C to 1,400°C).

According to Peterson, "The Chinese were the first to build kilns that would reach 2400 degrees F (1300 degrees C)."[20] It was also in East Asia that the oldest pottery-making culture, the Japanese Jomon, was discovered.

East Asia

It is in the Far East—primarily China, Korea, and Japan—that the earliest innovations in virtually all stages of the potter's art can be found.

—Prudence M. Rice, *Pottery Analysis*

Vast improvements in the process of creating and decorating pottery began in the countries of East Asia, especially China, Japan, and Korea. China led the way with the development of porcelain and numerous technical and artistic innovations that influenced pottery making in its neighboring countries and in much of the world. China's regional neighbors, Japan and Korea, also developed specific pottery traditions. The island-nation of Japan created Jomon ware, the oldest carbon-dated pottery in the world.

Ten Thousand Years of Jomon

The porous, coiled earthenware pottery of Japan called Jomon spanned more than ten thousand years, from about 12,000 B.C. to 2000 B.C. The term *Jomon* means "cord mark" in Japanese and refers to the distinctive pattern made by pressing cord or rope onto the surface of the clay as decoration. The initial and early Jomon pottery period (ca. 12,000–10,000 B.C. and 6000–

4500 B.C., respectively) was "dominated by deep vessels that are fundamentally of 'flowerpot' shape," writes Jomon historian C. Melvin Aikens, "with broad open mouths and straight walls that taper slightly inward toward a flattened base."[21] During the middle Jomon period (ca. 4000 B.C.), decorations such as serpents and other animal heads wound around the rims of the pottery. They were so elaborate that some became unbalanced and top-heavy.

Late Jomon (ca. 3000 B.C.) was distinguished by what Aikens calls "zoned cord marking, in which patterns outlined by deep incising or grooving were filled with cord marks."[22] By the final Jomon period (ca. 2000–300 B.C.) the pottery was noted for its burnished surfaces.

The Jomon people were at first hunters, gatherers, and fishers. As more immigrants began to arrive in Japan from the mainland, a new culture developed that focused on the cultivation of wet rice as a food source. The shift from hunting and

While originally made for functional use, during the middle Jomon period, this deep Jomon bowl (c. 4000 B.C.) also was used for social rituals and to display an individual's social status.

gathering to an agricultural society resulted in different types of vessels and improved pottery techniques.

Progress in Pottery

The spread of agriculture, the use of primitive wheel turning in the making of pottery, and the start of metalworking characterized the Yayoi period in Japan (ca. 300 B.C. to A.D. 300). Yayoi potters created new vessels for boiling, cooking, and

During the Haniwa period (about A.D. 200 or 300 to 600) these figures were placed in the ground around a person's tomb to serve as guardians.

storing rice. They were smoother, more balanced pots, produced with a potter's wheel and fired at higher temperatures that made the red-orange pottery less porous.

Successive periods in Japan were noted for technological advances in pottery making and unique and interesting clay vessels and figures. During the Haniwa or Tumulus period (ca. A.D. 200 or 300 to 600) clay figures were placed around tombs in underground burial chambers. Called Haniwa figures, they served as guardians for the dead. According to Nelson and Burkett, "the first Haniwa were simple clay cylinders. Later ones were more elaborate representations of armored warriors, robed ladies, horses, and other attendant figures."[23]

The Japanese also made progress in the firing of pottery by adopting anagama kilns from the Koreans and the Chinese. These tubelike chambers were constructed on the slope of a hill and allowed higher temperatures to build up for the firing. It often took many days for the kiln to heat up to the firing temperature and then cool down again. Being able to create these higher temperatures was important to the development of stronger, higher-quality pottery. In the centuries that followed, changes to the types and quality of pottery desired were inspired by the acceptance and growth of Buddhism. Buddhism changed many facets of Japanese society, including pottery making.

Buddhism, Lead Glaze, and Pottery Centers

Shinto was Japan's native religion, but when Buddhism was introduced in the sixth century from China and Korea, it was quickly accepted by the ruling class as the new state religion in Japan. Once Buddhism was accepted, Chinese culture began to influence all aspects of Japanese life. This included more sophisticated pottery techniques. Chinese lead-glazed pottery became popular in Japan in the seventh century as did multicolor glazes in the eighth century. However, by the tenth and eleventh centuries Chinese influence had declined, and Japanese characteristics reasserted themselves in the form of what Cooper explains were "quieter, softer ash-glazed wares, such as bottles with incised floral designs."[24]

The native religion of Japan is Shinto, which worships ancestors, tradition, the family, cleanliness, and nature. Shinto deities are called kami and are guardians who protect the people. Buddhism is a path of spiritual development attained through the use of meditation, nonviolence, and tolerance in order to nurture and promote qualities of kindness, wisdom, and compassion. Confucianism consists of teachings based on morality and ethics that include proper standards of behavior, righteousness, and honesty. Taoism is a way of life that rejects hatred and intolerance and exemplifies love, learning, and harmony in the world of nature.

By the fourteenth century, pottery production centers were established in locations throughout Japan, and each developed its own particular specialty. According to Charleston, the potters in Seto made "vases, bottles, and jars with pleasing streaky yellowish-green or caramel-brown glazes covering incised or stamped floral motifs."[25] The Tamba region became known for its tea ware. Thick and coarse Shigaraki pottery, write editors Lorenzo Camusso and Sandro Bortone, "became renowned for cups and bowls with characteristic, white, granular flaws resulting from impurities in the local clay."[26]

Tea for Two—Do You Raku?

Pottery objects used in the tea ceremony, such as tea bowls, incense holders, flower vases, cake trays, and water containers were in high demand. The tea ceremony originated within monasteries of the Zen sect of Buddhism. The ceremony, started by monks when they took breaks in their meditation, became a popular public ritual from the late fourteenth century onward.

The raku technique was developed especially for producing tea ware and is still used today. A glazed piece of pottery, made from large-grained coarse clay, is fired quickly in a kiln and then removed and rapidly cooled. Writer and ceramicist Polly Rothenberg describes the process:

> A . . . clay form is covered with a glaze that fuses from approximately 1600 degrees F to 1800 degrees. When the glaze is thoroughly dry, the object is put into a hot kiln. . . . The glaze firing is observed . . . until it starts to melt and turn shiny. The piece is pulled from the hot kiln. . . . As soon as its bright orange heat turns to dull red (in a matter of seconds), it is thrust into a container of . . . sawdust, pine needles, or dried leaves. . . . The lid is clamped on quickly to shut off oxygen in the air and make a reduction atmosphere. After . . . about three minutes, the piece is removed . . . and quenched in a bucket of water to "hold" the effects of reduction.[27]

The level of impurities in the clay, the ingredients used in the glaze, and the amount of oxygen the potter allows in the cooling process result in a unique appearance and variation of color in each finished raku piece.

Discovery of Kaolin and the Production of Porcelains

The Chinese had been manufacturing porcelain for many years by the time the Japanese discovered deposits of kaolin clay at Arita on the island of Kyushu in the early seventeenth century. The first Japanese porcelain, known as Imari ware and produced mainly for export, was decorated in blue and white. Later pieces were multicolored with detailed decoration in a variety of bright colors. By the middle of the nineteenth century, most of the pottery in Japan was produced for export and used simple designs created for mass appeal. Individual artists, however, kept alive the evolving art and technique of Japanese ceramics.

Advancements from China in the production and development of pottery cannot be underestimated. From earliest times

Most of the earliest Japanese porcelain, like the Ko-Imari bottle from the late seventeenth century pictured here, was produced in order to export to other countries.

and throughout the succession of powerful dynasties that ruled the country, pottery was highly valued.

China's Earliest Pottery

The Yellow River valley in northern China was home to much of the early Chinese pottery, dating around 5000 to 2000 B.C. Most pieces from this area were simple coil-built earthenware vessels of red clay obtained from the banks of the Yellow River. The coils of clay were stacked, pressed, and shaped by hand.

The Yang-Shao cultures of Kansu Province in central China had two basic pottery types dating from as early as 5000 to about 2000 B.C. The hand-built Pan-shan vessels were made of fine clay with thin walls and a smooth surface. Pan-shan jars and bowls were painted with crisscross lines, swirling patterns, and checkered-square decorations in red and black slip. Lung-shan wares were the first vessels in China produced on an early form of potter's wheel. They were distinguished by their thin walls, glossy black color, banded decorations, and variety of shapes, such as pots, urns, bowls, and other containers.

After around 1600 B.C., historical eras in China are divided into dynasties of ruling families and groups. These dynasties spanned periods of upheaval when independent Chinese states fought against each other, then reunited in a strong central government that promoted trade. Many of the dynasties offered something unique in pottery achievement and development. The first dynasty is called the Shang, and it lasted from 1766 to around 1122 B.C.

CLAY GUARDIANS OF AN EMPEROR'S TOMB

In 1974 Chinese well workers in X'ian accidentally came upon the tomb of Emperor Ch'in Shih Huang Ti or Shih Huang-ti (259 to 210 B.C.). A huge underground room was also discovered that contained six to eight thousand life-size clay warriors and their horses that served as guardians to the emperor in the afterlife. According to ceramic analyst and professor Prudence M. Rice,

The terra-cotta army was formed in separate pieces but without molds. Solid or hollow legs support hollow torsos made of coils of clay; heads, arms, and legs were shaped separately, then attached to the bodies with strips of clay; individualized facial features and costume details were sculpted . . . to finish the pieces before firing, then after firing the pieces were painted with red, green, black, and other colors.

Prudence M. Rice, *Pottery Analysis*. Chicago: University of Chicago Press, 1987, p. 15.

Glazes and Kiln Development

The first feldspathic glaze occurred during the Shang dynasty and combined feldspar and wood ash. When mixed together they produced greenish pottery glazes. Lead-silicate glazes of green or brown were introduced from Egypt and the Middle East during the Han dynasty (206 B.C. to A.D. 220). Chinese potters used them in funerary pieces, such as urns that held the ashes of the dead or pottery that was buried with the deceased in the tomb.

Improvements in kiln design allowed clay to be fired to much higher temperatures that resulted in harder and less porous pottery pieces. Cooper describes the kilns of this period: "[They] were built into the side of a hill and the heat rose up the kiln, with the result that higher temperatures were achieved near the fire-box at the bottom of the kiln and lower [temperatures] further up the kiln. . . . Kilns could be fired in which the hot areas were used for stoneware and the cooler areas for the lead-glazed earthenware."[28]

By the end of the Han dynasty, pottery making became localized in separate warring states. It was not until the Sui dynasty (A.D. 581 to 617) that China reunited and the trade routes reopened. This led to great accomplishments in the arts, literature, and ceramics during the following Tang dynasty.

Three-Color Tang and White Ware

The Tang, or T'ang, dynasty (618 to 907) was marked by increased trade and visitors from other countries, such as Mesopotamia, Persia, and India, which influenced Chinese pottery making. Cooper writes that "T'ang forms generally are characterized by a full, swelling, almost bursting body, contrasted with a light, fairly narrow neck. . . . Decoration was bold and assertive, and was modeled, incised, stamped or painted."[29]

A popular decorative style at this time was Tang three-color ware, which was actually more than just three colors. According to Camusso and Bortone, this style included shades of green from copper oxide, amber yellow to brown from iron oxide, blue from cobalt oxide, and purple from manganese.[30] These colored

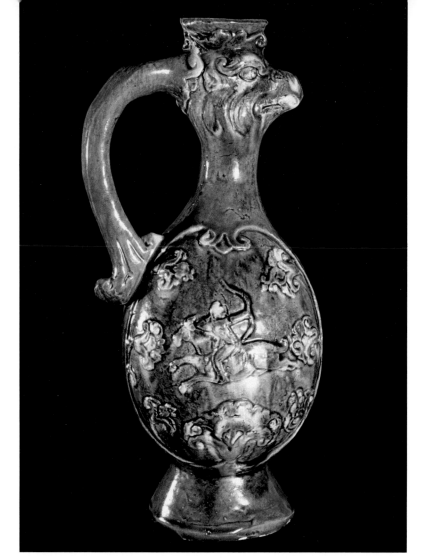

This phoenix-headed ewer shows the full body and narrow neck, which is characteristic of the Tang dynasty.

glazes were splashed, dripped, smeared, or painted onto the pottery surfaces. Frequently, the glazes were allowed to run down the vase or jug and merge together.

The most desirable vessels were pure white, which was the Chinese color for mourners and used in burial ceremonies. Many white-colored wares were produced, but it is not known now if they were true porcelains. The Tang dynasty ended in 907 and was followed by fifty years of unrest until China was reunited again under the Sung dynasty. The Sung dynasty brought new innovations to the art of pottery making, including the production of the finest pottery—true porcelain.

A Variety of Wares

Many types of pottery were produced during the Sung dynasty (960 to 1280), and an increased number of kilns allowed for more experimentation with metals and colored glazes. Sung potters found that the reduction of oxygen in the kiln at certain points during the firing changed copper glazes to various shades of red and iron-based glazes to shades of green and blue, which imitated colors in nature.

Rice explains that it was also during this period that "white, hard, translucent, and resonant porcelain reached its finest development."[31] The word *porcelain* originated with the explorer Marco Polo, who traveled to China in 1292. He described the white pottery in Italian as "alla Porcella—having the appearance of a delicate, shiny seashell."[32]

A well-known ceramic of this period was a type of white porcelain called Ting ware. Bowls, dishes, plates, jars, and pots were coated with ivory glaze. According to Cooper, "three different colours were made: pai-ting was brilliant and white, fen-ting had the colour of ground rice, while t'u-ting had a coarser body and a yellower glaze."[33] The rims were not glazed but banded with copper. Flower, dragon, or fish decorations were pressed or cut directly onto the surface.

The rarest pottery during the Sung period was Ju ware, which was made for the royal court in the early twelfth century. Ju ware forms were relatively simple. Charleston describes it as having a "highly refined, light bluish-green glaze . . . intentionally marked with a light 'crackle' of 'broken ice' fissures."[34] The Sung dynasty ended in the late thirteenth century. Next, China was dominated by the Mongol-controlled Yuan dynasty (1289 to 1367) formed by Kublai Khan. Pottery exports and trade increased to meet foreign demand, but styles remained the same until the mid-fourteenth century. A new white porcelain with blue or red decoration became popular when Chinese rule was reinstated with the Ming dynasty (1368 to 1644) and direct trade with Europe began (in 1517).

The Ming Porcelains and Increased Exports

Pottery production during the Ming period focused mainly on the new porcelains, made possible with imported cobalt oxide pigment from Persia, called "Mohammedan blue."[35] According to author David W. Richerson, the famous Ming vases "were made of fine white porcelain decorated with intricate scenes and designs. . . . A special slip containing the chemical cobalt oxide . . . was delicately painted onto the surface of the porcelain and coated with a glaze. During firing, the cobalt oxide turned . . . a permanent blue, and the glaze became a bright, colorless varnish."[36]

Another Ming dynasty achievement was the discovery of a copper red color, which occurred when a thin wash of copper oxide was applied over a glazed form and then fired in a reducing kiln. The result was multicolored shades of red pottery, often with fish or fruit decoration.

Painting with colored enamels also became popular during the Ming dynasty. These are multicolored glazes that were

This Ming dynasty porcelain jar displays the blue colors that were formed by cobalt oxidization during the heating process.

painted on already fired and glazed pieces and then fired again in a low-temperature kiln. The Ming influence on pottery ended around the mid-seventeenth century, when the Ming dynasty fell to the neighboring Manchurian Tartars who took control of the Ching dynasty, which lasted from 1644 to 1912.

Cooper notes that during the Ching dynasty Chinese trade flourished with countries such as Holland, Spain, Portugal, England, France, Denmark, and Sweden. European collectors of Chinese porcelain favored certain shapes and decorations, and the potters met these demands for export. Color combinations of green, yellow, and red were often used with decorations of flowers, birds, plants, and landscapes, sometimes with poems and inscriptions as well as animal and human figures.

Another country in East Asia to develop its own unique pottery styles and techniques was Korea. China influenced pottery styles and methods in Korea as well.

Similarities and Differences

Early Korean burial ware, such as cremation urns, was similar to that of China. Cooper writes that "jars . . . cups and food bowls were made and mounted, rather elegantly, on hollow stems which were often split and carved."[37] He notes that the best Korean pottery were celadon (light yellowish green) glazed pots, which were frequently tinted blue.

A distinctive form of Korean ware, writes Charleston, "is a technique of decoration first incised, then inlaid in white and black slips under the celadon glaze."[38] This inlay technique was known as mishima.

As pottery making developed in East Asia, it also thrived simultaneously in the Near and Middle East, first in ancient cultures and then under Islamic rule.

The Near and Middle East

One should never lose sight of the fact that these forms of pottery were as much the expression of a society as of an individual.

—Robert J. Charleston, *World Ceramics*

The ancient Near and Middle East included the countries of Mesopotamia (now Iraq), Persia (now Iran), Syria, Anatolia (now Turkey), and Egypt. All of the earliest forms of pottery from this region are simple, coiled vessels. Over time, the potters' techniques evolved into more advanced methods of form and decoration. According to Nelson and Burkett, "Despite regional variations, certain characteristics remained constant. . . . The use of repetitive patterns and symmetrical composition. . . . A preference for curved forms . . . [and an] emphasis on bright color."[39] The emergence of Islam in the seventh century and the empire that developed, changed not only the politics and culture, but many aspects of art in this part of the world, including pottery.

Starting Simple

Clay vessels from as early as 8000 to 6000 B.C. were discovered at Çatal Huyuk in Anatolia. "The pottery was of the simplest kind," writes art historian A.M.T. Moore, "consisting of deep bowls and hole-mouth jars, light in color and with burnished surfaces. Later on," he continues, "darker, harder-fired vessels were made, though the surfaces of nearly all of them were undecorated."[40]

According to Rice, "The earliest vessels in the Near East were hand built . . . then scraped, paddled, or rubbed to produce an even finish; they were fired without kilns in open bonfires, using wood or dung cakes for fuel. These . . . vessels come in a range of shapes, including bowls, cups, and trays."[41]

Pottery Advances in Mesopotamia

During the Halaf period, colors on painted decorations, such as the bowl pictured here, survived the firing process due to advances in kiln development.

Ancient cultures in Mesopotamia made two distinct types of pottery: bowls and rounded jars with plain engraved line patterns, and vessels called Samarra ware in which the decoration was painted on rather than engraved. Artists who produced Samarra ware painted geometric patterns as well as human and animal figures in red or black on light-colored vessels around 5000 B.C.

THE ISHTAR GATE

Decorative ceramic tile and brick were used extensively in the Near and Middle East in mosques and other buildings. One of the best examples is the Ishtar Gate of the ancient city of Babylon in Mesopotamia, built during the reign of Nebuchadrezzar II (604–562 B.C.). This main gate to the city was reconstructed from fragments found at the site by the Pergamon Museum in Berlin.

Forty-seven feet (14m) high and more than thirty feet (9m) wide, the gate is made of multicolored glazed clay bricks and tiles with raised relief patterns of dragons, lions, and bulls. These yellow and brown creatures are set among bright blue ceramic tiles and other intricate tile patterns.

The inscription by King Nebuchadrezzar reads, "I placed wild bulls and ferocious dragons in the gateways and thus adorned them with luxurious splendor so that people might gaze on them in wonder."

Bible History Online, "Ancient Babylonia: The Ishtar Gate." www.bible-history.com/babylonia/BabyloniaThe_Ishtar_Gate.htm.

This portion of the reconstructed Ishtar Gate, built during the reign of Nebuchadrezzar II (604–562 B.C.), is one of the best examples of decorative ceramic tile and brick used in Middle Eastern mosques and buildings.

The Halaf period in Mesopotamia, about 4500 to 4000 B.C., was noted for advances in kiln development that allowed colors on painted decorations to survive firing. Early kilns, in which the flame and smoke touched the pottery, made the colors appear cloudy. Mesopotamians produced a two-chamber kiln in which the pottery was kept separate and untouched by the flame and smoke, so the final product retained the vivid colors and contrasting designs painted on the pottery before firing. Halaf artists modeled much of their work after metal and bronze containers that were popular at the time. The round-bodied vessels often had curling rims and thin walls.

About 4000 to 3500 B.C. the slow potter's wheel developed in the Middle East, resulting in more uniformly shaped and finely made pottery. By 2000 to 1500 B.C., glass and then glazes were produced. Mesopotamians discovered that by adding lead, a glaze could successfully adhere to the clay. Lead and alkaline glazes made from sand and potash were frequently used, but they originated in Egypt.

THE INDUS CIVILIZATION

Potters of the Indus River valley (ca. 3000–1500 B.C.) in what is now northern India and Pakistan used a unique wheel which was set in a pit and is still used in some areas today. "The arrangement of the wheel consists of a pit in which is set a central axis connecting a heavy fly-wheel at the base with a lighter wheel-head at the top, on which the pots are made," historian and potter Emmanuel Cooper states. "The potters sit on the edge of the pit pushing and controlling the fly-wheel with their feet."

According to Cooper, the large cities of Harappa and Mohenjo-dara had "running water and sanitation." The residents developed the new crop of cotton, domesticated oxen, and used a form of irrigation for their crops. Cooper notes that broken pots found near a water source may indicate that the pots were "used once for drinking and then thrown away." If that was the case, he declares, "Such pots must have been produced both quickly and cheaply by the potters."

Emmanual Cooper, *A History of World Pottery*. Radnor, PA: Chilton, 1991, pp. 25–26.

The Land of the Pharaohs

Peterson writes that "the earliest glazes have been discovered in the Nile Valley of Egypt, dating from about 5000 B.C."[42] She notes that the early Egyptian glazes were a type of paste made from soda and silica, the ingredients of glass, but did not bond well with the clay. Early glazes were attempts to copy the blue color of the gemstone lapis lazuli. The glazes were used in making beads, tiles, and jewelry, but not used in pottery until about 1500 B.C.

The Egyptian Badarian culture, about 4000 to 3200 B.C., produced pottery that "gives a sense of restraint and simplicity which has rarely been equaled,"[43] writes Charleston. Using red Nile clay, the potters made strong, thin-walled pieces, including bowls with flat bases, and beakers with rims that spread outward.

Nelson and Burkett describe the production process: "Because the pots were fired upside down in little more than a bonfire, the upper rims of the red clay pots were covered with ashes and in direct contact with the burning coals." They continue, "This reduced the amount of oxygen and caused them to turn black, while the balance of the pot, exposed to the oxidizing effect of the air, retained its original red color."[44] Cooper refers to these tall jars and beakers as "black-topped red wares."[45] Egyptian pottery was influenced by the ceramics of other countries. As foreign trade increased, potters imitated the styles of imported wares.

"The Ancient Near East was never at any period a unified area, made up as it was of a diversity of peoples, economies and geographic environments,"[46] writes Charleston. That changed in the seventh century A.D. with the rise of the Islamic empire.

Islamic Pottery

The founder of Islam, the prophet Muhammad, died in A.D. 632. Over the next hundred years, his followers blazed a trail of conquest over Syria, Egypt, Persia, and Mesopotamia; parts of India and China in the east; and North Africa and Spain in the west. "Mohammad declared that the Koran was not only the word of God but a guide to the way of life," explains Cooper, "and forbade its use in translation; thus a single language was introduced which could be read throughout Islam and this had the effect . . . of unifying diverse peoples."[47]

As this Syrian earthenware vase from the fourteenth century shows Islamic potters experimented with the use of metallic decorations and glazes in place of gold and silver.

The victorious Muslims first absorbed and then advanced the artistic traditions of the areas they controlled. The Greek and Roman art influences in Syria and Egypt (which had been part of the Roman Empire) combined with what Cooper writes was "repeating symmetrical patterns with a strong abstract tendency"[48] from Mesopotamia. These merged together to form the arabesque style, described by Nelson and Burkett as "the flowing, interlaced curves of symmetrical floral motifs."[49]

Historians differ as to whether Islam actually forbids the use of human or animal figures in art. No reference to this is in the Koran, but it is mentioned in the Hadith, a holy book that contains the sayings of the prophet. Charleston writes that "the potter's art was hardly affected by this prohibition, Islamic pottery being used only for secular purposes until the thirteenth and fourteenth centuries."[50] Islam also forbids the use of precious metals like gold and silver in household or decorative objects, so potters experimented with the use of other metallic decorations and glazes as substitutes.

Strong Chinese Influences

As trade routes grew between the Far East and the Islamic empire, pottery styles and techniques in the Near and Middle East were influenced by Chinese potters after the eighth century. However, pottery was not state-sponsored, and ceramics were not made for the sake of art alone, as in China. Cooper writes, "All pots made by the Islamic potters had a use, mostly in the daily life of a Muslim, and qualities in the pots were rarely made just for their beauty."[51]

Unglazed wares were produced throughout the Islamic empire in a variety of shapes, sizes, and decorations. Muslim potters could not duplicate true porcelain because they lacked the necessary kaolin deposits that were available to the Chinese in great quantities, but they did produce glazed white wares that gave the appearance of porcelain.

Islamic potters copied the lead-glazed splashed pottery of the Tang dynasty in the ninth century. Red clay was used to form the piece, which was then covered with a white slip. Lead glaze in yellow, brown, green, black, or purple was applied to the pottery, then became fluid in the kiln and ran down the pot. The potters improved on the Chinese splashed wares by adding sgraffito designs under the glaze. This was, according to Cooper, "the technique of scratching a pattern through a clay slip of contrasting colour, usually white, to show the dark body beneath."[52]

Tin Glazes and Lusterware

What Charleston calls "opaque white tin-glazed painted pottery"[53] began to be produced in the ninth and tenth centuries. Muslim potters added tin oxides to lead glazes to create a white porcelain-type look to the pottery surface. This technique of tin glazing eventually spread throughout the Islamic world into Spain and Europe. Not content to leave the pieces undecorated, they painted designs of various colored pigments, including cobalt oxide, which produced the blue color of Chinese porcelain. Kufic inscriptions, a type of Islamic handwriting, were often painted on pottery as a decoration. Charleston writes that "The Kufic inscription most commonly found is the repetition of the word baraka (blessing)."[54] In Persia, Cooper writes, "simple bands of designs in kufic script were painted on to the white pot, often round the rim. . . . Such phrases as 'Generosity is (one) of the qualities of the blessed,' . . . or 'Good fortune' were used."[55]

One of the most notable technical accomplishments of Muslim artists was the creation of lusterware, which, Peterson notes, was a partial result of the ban on

This eleventh-century Iranian earthenware bowl bears kufic script, which Muslim potters used as a way to decorate pieces of pottery.

precious metal in Islam. Charleston describes the luster technique: "Metallic pigments are painted over a white opaque tin-glaze. . . . This . . . results in a surface which produces glittering reflections. The lustrous pigment was fixed on the glaze by a second firing under reducing conditions, after which a thin metallic film appeared evenly over the surface."[56]

Camusso and Bortone write that the technique of lusterware "reached its greatest heights during the twelfth and thirteenth centuries."[57] The center of lusterware production was in Kashan in Persia, where what was called the monumental style featured human or animal figures. The later miniaturist style consisted of smaller, more detailed designs that, according to Cooper, "was scratched through the painted lustre before it was fired."[58]

In the eleventh century Seljuk Turks from Central Asia, who had accepted Islam, invaded Persia, Mesopotamia, and Syria and established control of the empire. Advances in pottery developed during Seljuk rule that included both new and improved methods and techniques of pottery making.

Seljuks Rule

Inspired by the Ting ware of China, Muslim potters invented soft-paste porcelain. Nelson and Burkett write, "Firing at a low temperature, this new body was composed of powdered silica sand and alkaline frit (melted, reground glaze) held together with a white clay."[59]

Cooper notes that the powdered silica was often crushed quartz pebbles, and the alkaline frit was a potash and borax mixture. "The result was a low-temperature, translucent soft-paste body . . . and quite a good imitation of genuine porcelain . . . [that was] strong when fired and allowed pots with thin walls to be made."[60]

Silhouette-painted wares, produced in Persia during the twelfth century, consisted of designs carved or painted under the glaze. The pottery was covered with a black slip and the designs were scratched through the slip. The piece was then coated with a turquoise or ivory glaze and fired.

Persian mina'i (enamel) decoration is a technique in which the various colors are painted over the glaze and made permanent by an additional firing at low temperature. "Minai painting in polychrome enamel over opaque white or turquoise glaze," write Nelson and Burkett, "represented in miniature scenes of horsemen, court life, and romantic legends."[61] The haft-rang technique, writes Cooper, "was a method of underglaze decoration in which pigment was painted directly on to the biscuit-fired pot which was then dipped into a clear glaze."[62]

In successive centuries, the Seljuks were conquered by the Mongols, who were eventually conquered by the Ottoman Turks. Pottery making in the Near and Middle East was soon dominated by the emergence of the Ottoman Empire from the fifteenth through the nineteenth centuries.

Isnik Ware

The main center of pottery making under the Ottoman Turks through the seventeenth century was at Isnik in Western Anatolia. Isnik ware included glazed tiles for mosques and palaces,

This ceramic foot basin, made in the Isnik style, may have been used to wash the feet of Ottoman sultan Suleiman II Qanuni.

as well as dishes, plates, jars, bowls, and lamps with white, blue, green, purple, and red decorations.

A type of Isnik ware, called Rhodian or Damascus pottery, was "characterized by a bright and richly painted decorative style painted on to a fine white clay slip and finished with a clear shiny transparent glaze,"[63] writes Cooper. Miletus was another type and consisted of white slip over red clay, painted in blue, black, or green. According to Cooper, "Patterns and designs were based on naturalistic renderings of . . . carnations, roses, tulips, and hyacinths, while borders were often filled with arabesques and scrolls."[64]

With the Safavid dynasty in Persia (1499 to 1736), several types of pottery had a revival, including soft-paste porcelain, celadon ware patterned after the Chinese green-glazed ceramics, and lusterware. Gombroon ware, shipped from the port of the same name, was exported to Europe and became very popular in England. "The pots were characterized by a fine, white, slightly translucent body," writes Cooper, "sometimes with pierced or incised decoration covered with a shiny glaze. Jars, bowls, plates and ewers [pitchers and jugs] with tapering spouts were made."[65] Kubachi ware "were large dishes and plates" of "dull red, brown, green, white, yellow and black . . . painted under a clear colourless crackled glaze,"[66] writes Charleston. Cooper notes that Islamic potters were strongly influenced by foreign ceramics but quickly adopted the forms and decorations for their own purposes.

Blue and white pottery production in the Near and Middle East competed for the European trade into the nineteenth century. However, the increased manufacture of pottery in Europe and the cheap production process of European porcelain resulted in the decline of Islamic pottery and a new focus on European goods.

Europe

Europe was not an independent center of pottery development.
—Prudence M. Rice, *Pottery Analysis*

European ceramics were greatly influenced by the early civilizations of Greece and Rome, as well as the styles and techniques of Chinese ceramics and Islamic ware from Spain. Evidence of prehistoric functional earthenware exists in Europe, but it is not of great importance in the evolution of European pottery, which traces its roots to Greece.

An Emphasis on Human Form and History

About 1000 B.C. the art and culture of classical Greece flourished. Most Greek pottery had a specific function, and the painted designs focused on daily life as well as past events. The potter's wheel was used extensively, and pots were often joined together in sections. Instead of glaze, a fine slip was used that became shiny after firing. In an oxidizing kiln atmosphere the clay fired red, while in a reducing atmosphere, the clay fired black.

Most Greek pottery held liquids ranging from wine and water to oil and perfume and were divided into several basic

A Greek vase painted using the red-figured technique. This style focused more on human figures than just decorations.

styles. The geometric style was distinguished by its attention to detail and patterns that included circles, lines, triangles, and squares. About 800 to 750 B.C. sticklike human and animal figures began to be used as decoration, and the pottery reflected the influence of Asian art. According to Nelson and Burkett, "Floral borders replaced the old zigzags, and stylized birds, animals, and finally figures from the Homeric legends filled the central panel."[67]

The black-figure technique (ca. 700–530 B.C.) was used on miniature vases and other small vessels. "Black silhouettes were drawn with a brush on the plain [red] clay ground," writes Charleston, "linear details then being added by incisions cut through the black before firing."[68] The red-figured style developed about 530 to 520 B.C., and the focus of decoration shifted to human beings. More depth and texture of the figures was added with three-quarter views and varied

THE MINOAN POTTERY OF CRETE

Early Minoan pottery (3000 to 1500 B.C.) was black with corded designs. Later, wheel-thrown pieces were decorated with geometric bands. Shapes ranged from wine and drinking cups to bowls, vases, and pitchers painted in white, red, blue, and black on dark and then lighter backgrounds. Three-footed mugs and three-handled pots with plant and sea designs were produced, as well as huge storage jars that contained wine and oil. These coil-built jars were close to 6 feet (1.83 m) tall and were adorned with rings and waves of rope decoration.

No human forms were painted on the unglazed Minoan pottery. Subjects were often stylized and abstract, then became more true to nature. Art historian and potter Emmanuel Cooper writes, "Vivid pictorial representations of plants, lilies, octopus, seaweed and marine life in general were painted with great vigour, often over the whole surface of the pot."

The Minoans traded frequently with the Greeks, and Cooper writes about a link between the two cultures. He states, "In Crete we see the beginnings of Greek shapes and Greek vase painting [but] there is none of the heaviness which Greek pots sometimes have." Most of Minoan society was destroyed about 1400 B.C. after a nearby volcanic eruption and subsequent tsunami.

A Minoan stirrup jar with octopus trademark, c. 1300–1200 B.C., received its name from the stirrup-shaped handles around the jar's false neck.

Emmanuel Cooper, *A History of World Pottery.* Radnor, PA: Chilton, 1991, p. 25.

spacing. Subject matter ranged from chariots and warriors to mythological figures.

At the same time that Greek culture was thriving, the Etruscans established city-states in an area near what is now Rome and Florence in Italy. The Etruscans traded extensively with the Greeks and were influenced by the geometric and red-figure pottery style. By the fifth century B.C. Roman tribes conquered the Etruscans and the Greeks, and by about 275 B.C. occupied the entire Italian peninsula.

The Crossroads of the World

At its height, the Roman Empire (30 B.C. to A.D. 476) included Spain in the west, Britain in the north, and all of the Middle Eastern and Mediterranean countries. The city of Rome was a bustling metropolis of one million people. The Romans imitated Greek ceramics but standardized it throughout the empire. They established pottery centers that mass-produced an inexpensive red-gloss ware. Clay with an added alkali was formed in carved molds and fired in oxidizing kilns that gave it a red color. "The decoration appeared in relief on the surface of the bowl,"[69] writes Cooper.

Plain and undecorated red-gloss pieces were made as domestic tableware and included dishes, cups, and bowls with potters' names or marks stamped on them. What was called coarse pottery was mass-produced for the lower classes for use in the kitchen. These wares had no surface treatment and were efficiently made in several basic forms for cooking and storage purposes. Lead-glazed pottery was also produced extensively. Cooper notes that the best of the red-gloss ware was Arretine pottery, made in the Roman city of Arretium.

The Romans introduced pottery production methods to all of Europe, but the collapse of the empire in A.D. 476 brought an end to most Roman ceramic techniques. However, lead glazing continued to be used in Byzantium, which was renamed Constantinople, and became the capital of the eastern portion of the empire in A.D. 330.

The Byzantine Empire flourished during the Middle Ages (about the fifth century to the fifteenth century). White-bodied ware was produced with painted designs in the form of animals, crosses, and human figures. Byzantine potters also created red clay vessels covered with a white slip and decorated with sgraffito designs, which were scratched through the slip to show the red color beneath.

The lead-glazed ware spread to medieval Europe because it was easy to produce using local clays. Meanwhile, the tin-glazed technique of the Islamic world, in which tin oxide was added to lead glaze, spread into Spain and then into Italy during the Renaissance (about the fourteenth through seventeenth centuries).

You Say Majolica, I Say Maiolica

Spanish potters adapted the Islamic technique in which, according to Cooper, "they used a white tin-glaze applied to biscuit fired pots and fired the glaze in a second firing. The surface was then decorated with designs in rich lustre and fired a third time."[70] These were called Hispano-Moresque wares and had predominantly Muslim designs. Outstanding among these pieces were the Alhambra vases, which stood about 4 feet (1.22m) tall and had wing handles and script decoration.

In Italy decorated pottery was imported from Spain and then imitated by Italian potters. Rice explains, "The type of pottery on which this [tin] glaze appears is a fine earthenware known variously as majolica or maiolica . . . after . . . an island from which the tin-glazed wares were shipped to Italy."[71]

Majolica decoration in the sixteenth and seventeenth centuries included painted scenes from the Bible or the classics. Some potters imitated works of the popular painters in Italy. "While forms generally became more complex and ornate they were often overshadowed by the decoration,"[72] writes Cooper.

Tin-glazed pottery was called faience in France since most pieces arrived from Faenza, Italy. The sixteenth-century French potter Bernard Palissy (1510–1590) became very well known for

Alhambra vases, such as the one pictured here, were amazing pieces of Hispano-Moresque wares because of their height, which was about 4 feet tall.

The Three Books of the Potter's Art— Li Tre Libri dell' Arte del Vasaio

Cipriano Picolpasso was a potter in the town of Castel Durante in Italy, which specialized in the production of maiolica/majolica as well as traditional pottery. He wrote *The Three Books of the Potter's Art* in about 1556, the first "how-to guide" on pottery published in Europe. Picolpasso described in detail the methods of clay preparation, wheel-throwing, glazing, painting, decoration, and firing processes of majolica.

Workshops existed in all the arts—for goldsmiths, painters, sculptors, clockmakers, carpenters, and metalworkers. Picolpasso described the potter's workshop that usually employed eight to ten people who were wheel throwers, painters, kiln workers, and general apprentices. He also noted what specific oxides to add to the clay to obtain certain colors—such as cobalt for blue, copper for green, tin for white, and antimony for yellow. The books are all fully illustrated showing busy potters using pedal-powered wheels to produce and decorate vases and dishes.

Ceramics Today, "Picolpasso and the Art of Majolica in 16th Century Italy—Part One." www.ceramicstoday. com/articles/011199.htm.

faience that used bright, multicolored glazes. Charleston writes, "Casts, taken from life and naturally reproduced, of snakes, lizards, frogs, fishes, shells and foliage, won him fame and in 1562 earned for him the title of 'inventor of the king's rustic pottery.'"[73] By the eighteenth century, the faience factory in Rouen developed its own style, called rayonnant, described by Charleston as a "rich embroidery of lines in blue on a white ground."[74]

Soft- and Hard-Paste Porcelain

The appeal of Chinese porcelain and the introduction and rapid popularity of coffee and tea drinks in France and the rest of Europe increased the demand for cups, pots, and containers made from this highly regarded ceramic. "Kaolin for making hard-paste porcelain was still unknown in France," writes Charleston, "but eventually ceramic experiments resulted in an artificial paste from which a 'soft' porcelain . . . could be made,"[75] fired at a lower temperature than hard-paste porcelain.

The production of soft-paste porcelain at Sèvres in the mid-eighteenth century was supported by the French royal family. According to Charleston, "Coloured grounds were to become more and more dominant, until they almost completely covered the fine white glaze."[76] Shades of blue, yellow, and bright pink were often used in these creations. Production of true porcelain did not occur until the discovery of kaolin deposits at Saint Yrieix. The manufacture of hard porcelain began in the late eighteenth century at the royal factories at Limoges and Sèvres.

The Netherlands and Germany

Tin-glazed earthenware became known in the Netherlands as Delft ware, for the town in which the factories were located. The Dutch attempted to imitate Ming blue and white porcelain as closely as possible. Charleston notes that a clear lead glaze known as kwaart gave the vessel an even shine and more depth to the colors.

Delft potters also produced vases and water jugs more than 3 feet (.91m) high for the English royal family. The creation of blue and white tin-glazed tiles, which were widely exported throughout Europe and frequently imitated, were used on walls or to form small decorative pictures.

Roman coarse pottery continued to be made in the area that is now Germany for use in the home. New rounded and pear shapes emerged in the ninth century and lead-glazed earthenware remained popular. Maiolica flourished in Germany and imitated Italian and then Delft ware in the Chinese style. Even after the discovery of hard-paste porcelain in Germany, maiolica factories "provided a cheaper but acceptable alternative,"[77] writes Cooper.

Improved kilns and higher temperatures brought about the development of harder stoneware pottery. German clay, which was gray and had a large sand content, could maintain its form even at high temperature firings. Although similar to porcelain,

A Bellarmine jug, embossed with the likeness of Cardinal Robert Bellarmine, and a seal below the face. This is an example of brown salt-glazed pottery produced in the late sixteenth century.

stoneware is not white-colored or clear. Since glazes could not withstand the high kiln temperatures, red clay washes were used as decoration.

Salt Glazing

In the late fourteenth century, sodium chloride, common salt, was thrown into the kiln and mixed with Rhineland clay that had a high silica content. Cooper explains, "The sodium combines with the surface of the clay to produce a chemically simple but extremely tough and resistant glaze."[78]

Brown salt-glazed pottery looked very much like bronze metalware and was used extensively. Pint-size drinking mugs were made as well as three-handled jugs 1 foot (.3m) high. "One of the major products were the . . . Bellarmines, full, round-bodied jugs with narrow necks," writes Cooper. "These were decorated with a grotesque bearded face modeled on the neck."[79]

White salt glaze was produced in the sixteenth century. Spouted jugs and tall, thin drinking vessels were made with detailed relief decorations, usually with religious subjects. In the seventeenth century, German potters started to use colors such as cobalt blue and manganese purple, and, eventually, enamel painting was adapted for salt-glaze pottery.

True Porcelain in Germany

According to Charleston, a young alchemist named Johann Friedrich Bottger and a physicist named Ehrenfried Walther, Count von Tschirnhaus, discovered hard-paste porcelain in Meissen, Germany, in 1708. At first, Oriental-type porcelain was produced, then other decorative styles were created with gold embellishments and colored enamels.

Johann Joachim Kandler took charge of the Meissen factory in 1733 and created large porcelain figures of lifelike animals, birds, characters in love, harlequins, and even beggars and other common people. He also designed dishes and utensils that were purchased by wealthy individuals. By the late eighteenth century, twenty-three factories produced Meissen-style porcelain in Germany.

Pottery developed later and more slowly in England because the country is separated from the European continent by the English Channel. The migration of what were called the Beaker people from Spain about 2000 B.C. or earlier accounted for large, hand-built, simple drinking cups with wide mouths and incised decorations found in England.

THE DISCOVERY OF PORCELAIN

A German alchemist named Johann Friedrich Bottger was supposedly successful at turning metal into gold. When the ruler of Saxony, Augustus the Strong, heard about this, he had Bottger imprisoned and ordered him to produce gold for the king of Prussia. After three years of failure, a well-known physicist named Ehrenfried Walther, Count von Tschirnhaus, started to work with Bottger on the project. While trying to turn metal into gold, they accidentally discovered hard red stoneware.

When the two men experimented with a white clay from the Meissen area (presumably kaolin) in 1708, they created hard-paste Chinese porcelain. "Meissen immediately became the envy of an astonished Europe and provided Augustus the Strong with a unique means of parading wealth and power," writes art historian Robert J. Charleston. "In 1710 he founded the Meissen manufactory which is still in production today." Charleston notes that on the entrance to his lab, Bottger had written the words, "God the Creator has made a potter out of an alchemist."

Robert J. Charleston, *World Ceramics*. Secaucus, NJ: Chartwell, 1968, pp. 216, 218.

Early Pottery in Great Britain

In A.D. 43 Roman conquerors brought advanced pottery production and decorative methods to Great Britain. They introduced Britain to the potter's wheel and improved kilns, as well as Roman red-gloss pottery and coarse, unglazed ware. When the Romans left in the fifth century, the pottery industry in Britain declined until trade with Europe picked up in the seventh and eighth centuries. The fast wheel was brought to the British eastern coast from Europe, and lead glaze was reintroduced.

From the eighth to the eleventh century, Ipswich ware, unglazed sandy, gray cooking pots, bowls, and spouted pitchers with applied decoration, was produced in Britain. Stamford pottery was made from local clay and fired to an off-white color in an oxidizing kiln atmosphere.

Plates and cups were not made in medieval Britain, but jugs, bowls, and pitchers were very popular items. Jugs were tall and slim in the thirteenth century, and smaller and rounder in the fourteenth and fifteenth centuries. By the sixteenth century, black-glazed wares and Tudor lead-glazed green pottery were being produced. According to Cooper, "Earthenware, fired only once and glazed with powdered galena [a lead ore] dusted on to the leather hard pots, continued to form the basis of much of the pottery made in England until the late eighteenth century."[80]

The Importance of Slipware

Nelson and Burkett write, "The majolica tradition was never significant in England. More important was slipware made chiefly during the seventeenth century in Staffordshire."[81] Slipwares were multicolored mixtures of clay and water that were poured or trailed onto the pottery for decoration. Staffordshire was the largest production center and often used white clay slip contrasted with a red or brown clay body.

In the late seventeenth century the Toft family of Staffordshire became famous for creating oversized dishes. Charleston writes, "These were some 17 to 22 inches in diameter and 3 inches deep, flat-based and with a broad, flat rim. The body was of red clay covered with a white slip . . . the rim usually be-

ing ornamented with a lattice formed of diagonally placed lines of the two contrasting red slip-colours."[82] The Toft name was often part of the pattern.

Slipwares were also made at Wrotham in Kent, where three-or-more-handled cups (called tygs), double-looped-handled vessels, and four-nozzled candlesticks were produced. "Handles made by weaving different coloured clays together were a distinctive feature of Wrotham ware,"[83] states Cooper. Other local potteries developed their own forms and styles of decoration.

Cream-Colored Ware, Josiah Wedgwood, and Industrialization

Tin-glazed pottery was produced in England in the seventeenth century mainly for its smooth white surface and

THE HEALTH RISK OF BEING A POTTER

Historian Bevis Hillier wrote about the life and status of those who worked with ceramics in eighteenth- and nineteenth-century England. "The potter's job was messy and unhealthy," Hillier explains. "His lungs were injured by clay dust, powdered flints, . . . calcined bones and sulphur fumes. He became rheumatic from exposure to high temperatures and rapid transitions of heat, and went blind from the glare of the ovens."

When potters worked with lead-glazed wares, they exposed themselves to lead poisoning through the fumes and dust of melted and ground metals and, according to J.T. Arlidge, who wrote a book on occupational diseases in 1892 from which Hillier quotes, "the immersion of the hands in the metallic solution." Women who cleaned the pots, Hillier states, "lived in a perpetual cloud of clay dust." Since coal was used to fuel the kilns, heavy coal dust and smoke was thick all around the potteries. Hillier notes that in the late nineteenth century the average life expectancy of potters was 46.5 years, while those in other occupations lived to an average age of 54. By the late nineteenth century, a British law banning the use of raw lead in pottery manufacturing was passed.

Some potters were so dedicated to their art that their judgment might be questioned. Supposedly, the French ceramist Bernard Palissy used the wood from his own furniture to fuel his kiln. According to Hillier, a potter named Pousa from China "threw himself into the oven when the last sticks of furniture had been burnt, to complete the firing of an exquisite bowl. The chemical reaction of his bones was said to have produced a glaze of unmatchable beauty."

Bevis Hillier, *Pottery and Porcelain, 1700–1914*. New York: Meredith, 1968, pp. 19, 21, 26.

resemblance to Chinese porcelain. However, the discovery of cream-colored ware by Josiah Wedgwood (1730–1795) replaced tin-glazed pottery by about 1800. The same clay used to create white salt-glazed ware was, according to Charleston, "low-fired to form an earthenware and glazed with lead instead of being high-fired to form a stoneware and glazed with salt."[84] He notes that it was sprinkled with powdered lead ore, then mixed with flint and fired. Unfortunately, the lead dust was toxic when inhaled by the potters, and this resulted in a serious health hazard. In the eighteenth century, creamware replaced the popularity of slipware in England and even faience and majolica in Europe.

Historians give Josiah Wedgwood most of the credit for the industrialization of the pottery industry in Britain. Peterson writes, "Wedgwood developed industrial production methods . . . shifting ceramics from small local potteries to large-scale industrial concerns producing quantities of cheap but high-quality ware for export as well as home use."[85]

Wedgwood produced green-glazed ware, unglazed black stoneware called basalts, pearl ware, and red stoneware. His famous jasperware was a white stoneware colored in pale or dark blue, green, lilac, or yellow with white-relief classical designs that stood out in contrast to the background colors. This cameo style pottery is still manufactured today.

After the discovery of soft-paste porcelain in France and hard-paste porcelain in Germany, English factories began to manufacture both types in the mid-eighteenth century. In 1800 the potter Josiah Spode added calcined bone ash to his formula for porcelain. The result was bone china, a very white, hard, translucent form of porcelain.

Response to Industrialization

The efficient mass production techniques of the industrial revolution made pottery available to everyone at affordable prices. The use of machinery, molds, and engraved metal plates "forced individual potters into large factories," state Nelson and Burkett, "where they performed a small, repetitive task in a huge mass-production enterprise."[86]

A commonly held belief was that the creation of art, which involved original expression and emotions, was separate from the production of crafts that were made through learned skills and techniques. A growing concern developed about

THE MARTIN BROTHERS' RESPONSE TO INDUSTRIALIZATION

These brothers did not make "traditional country pots or industrial wares," writes historian and potter Emmanuel Cooper. In response to the Industrial Revolution in England, Robert Wallace Martin (1843–1923) and his three brothers, Charles, Walter, and Edwin, designed and produced their own pieces in a studio in Southall, Middlesex, in 1877.

Cooper describes their pottery: "The pots were saltglazed in subdued colours, with painted oxides used to give dark blue, purplish-brown and dark brown. Decorative vases and jugs were made with relief, incised or painted decoration, as well as fireplaces and fountains, chess sets and some tableware." A distinguishing feature of this pottery was "face jugs and pots in animal form."

Emmanuel Cooper, *A History of World Pottery*. Radnor, PA: Chilton, 1991, pp. 167–69.

commercialization and profit at the expense of workmanship and the artist's craft. Protest and reaction grew in the form of the Arts and Crafts movement, which promoted art for its own sake and beauty over function. A key figure in this movement was the English designer William Morris (1834–1896) who believed that art and craft could not be separated. Some factories responded to the protests and developed separate art departments and hired outside designers. Some potters like the Martin brothers in England worked in their own studios.

By the late nineteenth century the Art Nouveau style was adopted by many artists, including potters who were influenced by Japanese techniques and focused on animal shapes and plant forms in nature. While European ceramics developed and advanced, potters in the Americas worked independently without benefit of glazes or the potter's wheel.

The Americas

Lacking the wheel and kiln, New World potters were rarely able to attain the same levels of technical achievement and standardized production as did their stoneware- and porcelain-producing Old World contemporaries.

—Prudence M. Rice, *Pottery Analysis*

Pottery developed independently in North and South America thousands of years later than in Asia, Europe, and the Middle East. Colored slips and paints were used on hand-built vessels that were baked in open bonfires. Most New World pottery was terra-cotta or earthenware because of the lack of high-firing kilns and clays. It was not until the sixteenth century that glazes, the potter's wheel, and kilns were introduced by European explorers and colonists.

Early Pottery in the Western Hemisphere

Most historians agree that the earliest known pottery in the western hemisphere dates from about 3200 to 2500 B.C. and was discovered on the coast of what is now Ecuador. Additional evidence of pottery from about 2500 to 2000 B.C. has been found

This Teotihuacan pottery vessel of a storm god, c. 150 B.C.–A.D. 750, shows the characteristic style of the curved bottom and three feet commonly found on the early pots made in the Americas.

in Mexico and Peru. These were relatively simple, thick, and compact forms made by coiling, hand modeling, or molds.

Most early pots in the Americas had curved bottoms or were three-footed, which was evidence that they sat on the ground on uneven or soft surfaces. "Faces modeled on pots point upwards so they can be clearly seen when the pots are sitting on the ground,"[87] explains Cooper. In addition to colored slips, decorations were incised or carved in relief. Patterns were commonly geometric or stylistic animals and flowers. Pottery was made for cooking or storage, religious uses, as toys or musical instruments, and as funerary urns.

Separate cultures in parts of Mexico and what is called Mesoamerica (middle or central America) developed their own pottery traditions. The Olmecs (ca. 800–400 B.C.) lived on the Gulf coast of Mexico and built pottery and pyramids dedicated to their jaguar god. "The naturalistic hollow pottery of this culture," writes Charleston, ". . . was characterized by mouths drooping at the corners."[88] Around the same time in the valley of Mexico, farm villages created clay figurines, and, according to Nelson and Burkett, "burnished black or red earthenware with simple, incised designs . . . [and] pots modeled in the form of birds or fish."[89]

Independent city-states existed peacefully until about A.D. 900 when a period of war, violence, and human sacrifice became prevalent. The large city of Teotihuacan consisted of pyramids, temples, and one-story structures decorated with murals. Nelson and Burkett note that the distinctive pottery in Teotihuacan "was a low, cylindrical ceremonial urn on three legs. The brown body was often cut away and coated with red pigment to leave a stylized raised design."[90]

From the Mayans to the Aztecs

Farther south in the area of Honduras and Guatemala, the Mayans flourished (ca. A.D. 250–900). Charleston calls them "the most advanced people of Ancient America with unrivalled achievements in astronomy, mathematics, writing, art and architecture."[91] Mayan potters produced a variety of forms and decorations described by Rice as "cylindrical vessels and plates [that] portrayed human and animal figures in a graceful natural style, featuring mythical and ritual scenes such as dances, processions, or royal audiences . . . painted with . . . sheer, glossy pale orange slip."[92] As the Mayan culture declined, the Toltecs began to thrive in the area and established the city of Tula. They produced a red and cream pottery and an orange and tan ware painted with wavy lines in what was called the Mazapan style. Another Toltec style, plumbate ware, was black and shiny.

The Aztecs ruled a vast empire in Mexico and Mesoamerica from about 1325 to 1520. They conquered and assimilated many other cultures, so their pottery reflected a wide range of styles and forms. However, they produced a distinctive orange ware with a black-lined painted decoration and a multicolored ware using yellow, red, gray, and black slips, decorated with human figures, feathers, and scrolls. Unfortunately, states Cooper, "They founded a society . . . involving horrible rituals in which priests carried out mass human sacrifices."[93] The arrival of Spanish explorer Hernando Cortés in 1519 resulted in the end of the Aztec Empire by 1521. On the Pacific coast of South America and in the Andes Mountains, other cultures independently developed unique styles in clay.

Early South American Pottery

The first pottery from Ecuador, dating from 3200 to 2500 B.C., was a black or gray corded ware with a curved bottom. A little later, the Chavin style (also known as Cuprisnique) was made around 800 B.C. and "was characterized by gourd-shaped pots in white or buff body sometimes decorated with a red inlay, topped by a stirrup handle,"[94] according to Cooper. These jars and pots often had a jaguar theme and incised patterned decoration. Some were modeled in the shape of a human face, animal, or vegetable. The stirrup handle looked like a saddle stirrup (that supports the rider's foot on a horse) with a pouring spout that rose straight up from the middle of the curve of the stirrup.

Stirrup bottles and vases were also representative of the Mochica culture (ca. A.D. 1–1200) This advanced people built irrigation systems, aqueducts, and sun-dried clay adobe brick structures. Charleston notes that many of their daily activities were drawn or painted on the pottery, "with excellent relief-modeling or vivid narrative scenes skillfully drawn in red on a cream background." He declares that "as a result . . . more is known about the Mochica than any other people before the Incas."[95]

Mochica pots were made in the shape of fruits, vegetables, faces, or animals from fired clay molds. Musical instruments such as the flute and trumpet were made from clay, and special clay jars shaped like birds whistled when liquid was poured from the spouts. After the downfall of the Mochica around A.D. 1200, the Chimu people flourished. The Chimu adopted much of the Mochica pottery tradition. At about the same time, the south coast Nazca culture thrived and developed a unique pottery type.

Nazca pottery was brightly colored in black, red, white, yellow, green, brown, pinkish/purple, and tan. Designs of people or animals were outlined in black on a red background. Double-spouted vessels with flat strap handles were produced. Later, jars were made in the shape of human faces and included mythological and religious themes. The Tiahuanaco people, who lived mainly in the Andes Mountains of Bolivia (about A.D. 1000) built tall, cylindrical pots, and, according to authors Nelson and Burkett, "flaring goblets, wide-rimmed bowls, and oval and modeled vessels with two spouts and a strap handle."[96] At about the same time, in the Chancay Valley of Peru, thin jars were made in egglike shapes with small human features applied in relief.

This brightly colored Nazca pottery displays the double spouts and flat strap handles that were common during the period.

The Inca Empire

Stretching nearly 400,000 square miles (1,036,000 square km) from high in the Andes Mountains of Peru to parts of Ecuador, Bolivia, Chile, and Argentina, the Inca Empire is considered one of the greatest world civilizations. From north to south, Charleston writes, "Their system of fortifications, roads, and bridges united an empire more than three thousand miles in length."[97] The mountain capital city of Cuzco was so rich in gold and silver that the walls of the Temple of the Sun were covered in gold and purposely made to reflect the blinding light of the rising and setting sun. In the temple gardens were gold statues of plants and animals. Successive outbreaks of European diseases like smallpox, typhus, and influenza brought over by the Spaniards wiped out more than 60 percent of the Incan population.

The Incan Empire attained the height of its power from the early fifteenth to the middle sixteenth century. The most distinctive of the Incan pottery was the aryballoid water jar, which had a long, narrow neck, pointed bottom, flared rim, and low handles on either side. It was produced in many sizes, and the largest was carried on a person's back with ropes threaded through the handles. Decoration was in the form of painted geometric shapes.

Communities in North America developed separate pottery traditions and art forms at the same time as the Central and South American cultures thrived. One of these was the Pueblo Indians in the American Southwest.

Early Native American Pottery

In the area of what is now Arizona and New Mexico, Indians lived in villages (pueblos) that consisted of adobe structures several stories high. Each tribe's pottery was distinguished from another's by its painted decoration. Zuni pottery was black and dark red on a pale gray background. The upper part of Acoma pots was painted with patterned floral bands in black and red. "At Santo Domingo a white slip background was decorated with pure geometric and more openly spaced black designs," writes Cooper. "Hopi pottery . . . was decorated with black designs on a yellow slip."[98]

Hohokam pottery, on the other hand, had no "decoration until A.D. 600–900 when red on buff painted bowls and jars carried animated, human and animal outlines,"[99] according to Charleston. A distinctive characteristic of Hohokam pots was a sharp shoulder where the rounded base met the straight sides of the vessel.

One of the most distinctive North American pottery types was Mimbres ware, made in southwest New Mexico. The black on white style consisted of painted decorations of people, animals, and other designs on the interior of the bowls. Pairs of insects, rabbits, or birds, spaced apart, were commonly painted on Mimbres ware. Funerary bowls buried with the dead had small holes in the bottom, supposedly to release their souls.

"In the southeastern and south-central United States," states Rice, ". . . decorative techniques, especially incising and modeling, rather than painting, were the outstanding modes of embellishment. Modeled heads of dogs or birds were often added to rims of simple globular vessels, or the vessels themselves might be in human or animal form."[100]

With the arrival of European colonists in the sixteenth and seventeenth centuries, the potter's wheel, kilns, and glazes

A Mimbres ware bowl, depicting a male and female, with a punctured hole in the bowl, from about the tenth century A.D. These bowls were presented as burial offerings, and the hole in the base of the bowl was to let the souls of the deceased escape to the afterlife.

were gradually introduced to the local populations. Pottery manufacture in the European style grew and evolved over time into unique American styles, although the wealthy continued to import higher quality ceramics from overseas.

American Folk Pottery

The simple designs and forms of folk pottery were made to fulfill particular functions or needs. They were to be used as cheese strainers, butter churns, chamber pots, milk pans, spice jars, pickle crocks, and bean pots. Low-fired and porous earthenware was produced from about 1640 through the 1780s, mainly in the New England colonies, while more durable stoneware was made from the early 1700s until about 1880 in New York and Philadelphia.

Early earthenware production was restricted to several basic shapes with simple line decorations. Powdered lead was sprinkled over the surfaces, making the vessels waterproof and creating a clear glaze. Later, pots were dipped into liquid lead

A Pottery in Colonial America

"The potter's workshop was usually a small shed near the house or attached to the back of the barn," writes art historian Harold F. Guilland. He describes one method in which two pits were dug adjacent to the workshop. In the first, fresh clay covered with water was mixed with a shovel. During the mixing, the rocks sank to the bottom of the pit and what remained was a smooth and consistent clay mix. The mix was then sifted through a sieve and 3 to 4 inches (7.62 to 10.16cm) was poured into the bottom of the second pit and allowed to dry. Succeeding layers were added and then dried into workable clay until the pit was filled. The clay was then cut into large blocks and stored in the potter's workshop.

Guilland also describes the early kilns used by colonial potters as

> a simple design with a longitudinal arch ten to twelve feet long built of brick. At the front of the kiln was a 2-foot opening which served as the fire mouth and door. At the far end there was a short [chimney] stack which created the draft. The floor was made of tamped earth and brick. Pots were stacked open on a raised platform in back of the firebox in direct contact with the flame. The kiln was fired for the day with wood from the nearby forest.

Early potters adopted the indentured apprentice system in which a young boy of around fourteen years of age "was bonded to the potter for a period of seven years or until he became twenty-one years old," writes Guilland. He was given a room, food, and clothing and taught to read or write, but the potter's apprentice worked long hours learning the tricks of the pottery trade. Once the apprenticeship ended, he worked as a journeyman potter and saved up his earnings to buy a shop of his own.

Harold F. Guilland, *Early American Pottery*. Philadelphia: Chilton, 1971, pp. 16, 18.

glazes. The pieces were commonly redware with a white slip, or sometimes yellow or brown. "Some potters . . . brushed coloring oxides on their ware," writes art historian Harold F. Guilland, "which blended with the glaze and flowed down the side of the pots adding complementary shading to the glazes."[101]

Most early potters were farmers who worked at making pottery part time. They used two types of wheels in producing vessels. The treadle or kick wheel was adapted from England and, according to Guilland, "was powered by moving a lever attached to a crank in the wheel shaft back and forth with the foot. The potter stood resting against the wheel, or leaning against the wall."[102] The Continental or kick and paw wheel was also foot powered. Guilland writes, "The potter sat on the wheel frame and pushed the heavy flywheel with his foot until it gained enough momentum to begin centering the clay with his hands."[103]

By the end of the American Revolution, potters were becoming aware of the dangers of lead glazes to good health. This health hazard, combined with the scarcity of costly European stoneware, resulted in a demand for the American manufacture of high-fired stoneware.

Stoneware Production

The production of stoneware required stronger kilns that could withstand the higher temperatures, 2,300°F (1,260°C), and depended on the availability of high-firing clays. Such deposits were discovered in the New York City and Philadelphia areas, which became important production centers for stoneware. The New York style, which spread north and westward, was, according to Guilland, "extremely well formed and finished. Elaborate decorative motifs were developed which were at first incised and later brushed and slip-trailed in cobalt blue slip." The Philadelphia style, which spread south and west, "was not . . . highly decorated."[104] Most stoneware was salt glazed, using the technique first introduced in Germany to avoid the lead-glaze hazard.

Frontier potters who lived in border settlements still produced earthenware because of the availability of red clay. However, as westward migration increased and transportation methods improved, stoneware potteries were eventually built. Potters began to

John Norton first made earthenware and then stoneware in Bennington, Vermont. Acclaimed potter Christopher Webber Fenton joined Norton pottery in 1837 and collaborated with Norton's grandson Julius to create Rockingham ware, which, historian and potter Emmanuel Cooper writes, was "characterized by a mottled brown glaze. Later this ware was improved by sprinkling different coloured oxides on the pots to give a blue, yellow, orange and green glaze mottled effect."

Fenton's partnership with Norton ended in 1847, and Fenton formed the United States Pottery Company in 1853, which produced a wide range of wares. According to art historian Harold F. Guilland, Fenton used kaolin (china clay) that had been discovered near Charleston, South Carolina. The company's wares included white and yellow earthenware, a type of porcelain called Parian that resembled marble, semiporcelains, and flint-glazed ware. Fenton sold coffee urns, foot baths, wash basins, spittoons, pitchers, teapots, cake pans, pie plates, candlesticks, picture frames, and doorknobs in various sizes. Guilland notes, "It is amazing that such a variety of objects and so many kinds of bodies and glazes should have been developed." This overproduction of goods may have helped to cause the downfall of the business in 1858.

A mottled brown glaze, a signature of Rockingham ware, covers this yellow earthenware pitcher.

Emmanuel Cooper, *A History of World Pottery*. Radnor, PA: Chilton, 1991, p. 163.

Harold F. Guilland, *Early American Folk Pottery*. Philadelphia: Chilton, 1971, p. 62.

work full time and moved west to take advantage of new markets and natural resources.

By the late 1830s the first European-style pottery factories were established in America. Mass-production techniques, using patterns and press molds, were introduced, bringing about the decline of American folk pottery. Major factories developed in Vermont and later in Ohio and other states. With industrialization came an increased focus on production and profits, and a decrease in quality and workmanship. However, some individuals were still interested in higher standards and a better caliber of pottery.

The Art Pottery Movement in Cincinnati

What started out as a hobby painting pottery led to the founding of Rookwood Pottery by Maria Longworth (Nichols) Storer in 1880 in Cincinnati. Storer's goal was to combine handcrafted ceramics with mass production methods. According to Camusso and Bortone, "Forms were thrown or moulded by potters and then decorated by other artisans. Thus the pieces, though handmade, were not the work of a single artistic sensibility."[105]

Rookwood ware was heavily influenced by Japanese pottery, which later evolved into Art Nouveau. Charleston writes, "Much . . . was decorated with asymmetrical arrangements of flowers painted in coloured slips beneath the glaze on a dark shaded ground. Great attention was paid to the figured grounds and glazes, which included such unique effects as 'tiger-eye,' a crystalline glaze introduced in 1884."[106]

Around 1900, other American potters produced ceramics with natural designs of plants and animals in the style of Art Nouveau. Women became more involved in pottery

The Japanese pottery style was a main influence in the look of Rookwood ware, such as this vase from potter Artus van Briggle in 1896.

COMMON AMERICAN POTTERY

Butter churns were popular and necessary pottery items in early America. They were tall jar-type vessels with a dasher (or plunger) at the top that moved up and down. Cream was placed in the churn, and the constant and steady action of the dasher made the cream foam and bubble. Then small pieces of butter formed and started to float to the surface. As the churning continued, the butter pieces stuck to each other and became larger lumps. The liquid buttermilk was then carefully strained out, and the butter was scooped out and salted.

Art historian Harold F. Guilland notes that "alcoholic beverages were considered a necessity rather than a luxury by early Americans." Salt-glazed stoneware jugs in assorted sizes were produced in large numbers to hold liquor. Liquor was not only used as a social beverage among adults, but for illness, as an anesthetic, for protection from the cold, and even for a snakebite. According to Guilland, "spirits were drunk . . . at meals, house and barn raisings, quilting bees, ordinations, weddings, funerals, political rallies, elections, trials, and militia trainings."

Harold F. Guilland, *Early American Folk Pottery*. Philadelphia: Chilton, 1971, p. 240.

making and decoration. Potters were gradually inspired to create art objects, not just functional wares. The artist-potters of the early twentieth century, in reaction to industrialization, began to create pottery in their own studios and carried out every level of production, from the digging of clay to the firing and decoration process.

6

The Emergence of Studio Potters

A potter on his wheel is doing two things at the same time. . . . His endeavor is determined in one respect by use, but in other ways by a never-ending search for perfection of form.

—Bernard Leach, quoted in the *Christian Science Monitor*, "East and West Melded in Spout and Lid."

The minute you touch a piece of clay it responds. It's like music.

—Peter Voulkos, quoted in Rose Slivka and Karen Tsujimoto, *The Art of Peter Voulkos.*

A multitude of studio artists working in clay emerged during the twentieth century. They produced pottery that ranged from functional domestic ware to nonfunctional abstract forms and sculptures that developed into a means of expression and art. The studio pottery movement and the establishment of ceramics as an academic discipline dominated the first part of the century, followed by increased experimentation in forms and glazes. Since the 1950s, traditional pottery techniques evolved into abstract expressionism and what was called the California Funk movement.

Most art historians agree that the main pioneer of the modern studio pottery movement in England and beyond was

Bernard Leach (1887–1979), who was greatly influenced by Japanese and other East Asian pottery techniques.

The Link Between East and West

Bernard Leach went to Japan in 1910 to teach drawing, but he became so interested in raku, the Japanese method of firing pots, that he decided to become a potter. He studied with the great Japanese master potter Kenzan VI and learned not only raku but stoneware firing at high temperatures. Leach returned to England in 1920. He was joined by the Japanese potter Shoji Hamada (1892–1978). Together they opened a studio pottery at St. Ives, Cornwall, England.

Leach produced low-priced domestic stoneware with brush-work, incised, and carved decoration. He combined Eastern techniques with traditional slipware. "Form . . . became his principal concern," states Cooper, "and the pots he made were conceived from an aesthetic as well as a functional point of view."[107] Leach's philosophy was to look to the East for inspiration. He worked with a team of potters and was involved in all processes of production. He wrote *A Potter's Book* in 1940, the first text that

This Bernard Leach earthenware dish with slip decoration, is an example of his style, which combines Eastern pottery techniques with traditional slipware.

dealt with philosophical as well as technical aspects of pottery. At St. Ives, Leach took on students, who developed and expanded upon his ideas.

Nazi Refugees and Leach Contemporaries

Two influential potters, Lucie Rie (1902–1995) and Hans Coper (1920–1981), were working in England around the same time. They had fled from the Nazis and settled in London. Rie came from Austria in 1938 and Coper came from Germany in 1939. They worked together from 1946 to 1958 and became lifelong friends. They frequently exhibited together, but their works were distinctively different from one another. When Rie first arrived in London, she was already an established potter, but her heavy-glazed, European-style pots were not well received. She tried to adopt Leach's studio pottery style, but was not successful.

During World War II Rie gave up pottery completely and produced ceramic buttons, jewelry, and umbrella handles for fashionable women's clothing designers. She gave Coper a job in 1946, and he encouraged her to resume her pottery career. After the war Leach helped them exhibit their work and gain recognition.

According to reviewer Janet Koplos,

> Rie's characteristic forms are an austere porcelain or stoneware bowl with a very small foot . . . or a long-necked vase with a rim so flared that it overshadows the rest of the bottle. . . . Her earliest work was burnished red earthenware. She later sgraffitoed the chalky surfaces of straight-walled bowls, gave rounder bowls brilliant green or blue glazes . . . or produced delicately colored, harshly pitted 'volcanic' textures."[108]

Koplos describes Coper's pots as "meldings of geometric shapes, such as a cylinder (the base), disk (the body) and cone (the neck and rim). His vessels have distinct fronts and backs and the arrangements of their parts may suggest figures. . . .

A porcelain bowl, created in 1924 by Adelaide Alsop Robineau, one of the few women at the time who was involved in every phase of pottery production.

He worked mostly in neutral colors or black and often abraded [roughened] the surfaces."[109]

Studio pottery also flourished in the United States in the early decades of the twentieth century. The United States also saw the establishment of formal ceramics training and publications that spread and shared knowledge among potters. Although he was often referred to as the father of American studio ceramics, Charles Fergus Binns (1857–1934) was born in England. By the time he immigrated to the United States, Binns was an accomplished potter and technician. In 1900 he helped found and was named director of the New York State School of Clay Working and Ceramics, which became the New York State College of Ceramics at Alfred University. Binns designed a practical and detailed curriculum that included all aspects of pottery making.

In addition to writing books and articles on pottery, Binns was the founder of the American Ceramics Society. As a practicing potter, he created ceramics in the style of the Ching dynasty and later worked with textured stoneware glazes. One of his students, Adelaide Alsop Robineau (1865–1929) also became prominent in the pottery movement.

At a time when many women were involved only in decorating and painting ceramics, Robineau was a studio potter involved in every phase of the production process. She threw her own pots, made her own glazes, and fired them herself. Although she focused on creating porcelain and studied Chinese techniques of firing at high temperatures, she also experimented with ceramic sculpture and other processes.

Robineau, who taught classes at Syracuse University, was interested in sharing ceramic techniques and information with other potters, and in 1899 she published and became editor in chief of a magazine called *Keramic Studio*, which became very successful.

A Myriad of Styles

By the mid-twentieth century, American ceramics came under the influence of several clay artists who fled from the Nazis in

PAINTERS INSPIRED BY STUDIO POTTERY

Famous painters such as Miró, Chagall, Léger, Matisse, and others have worked with clay. The most famous was Pablo Picasso, who began working with ceramics in 1947 at a pottery in France. "Recognizing that it would take a lifetime to learn to throw and glaze well," writes artist and educator Susan Peterson, "Picasso utilized glaze chemists and the throwers of the Madoura pottery at Vallauris. He reshaped the thrown plastic forms, or used the shapes of heavy clay products such as waterpipes; incised and painted them with enamels and experimental englobe colors; and applied glaze selectively." Picasso worked with earthenware and used bright, decorative colors. He painted vases, added images to traditional plates, and produced more than three thousand ceramic pieces throughout his lifetime. Peterson notes that what Picasso accomplished in ceramics "broadened the boundaries of what could be conceived and executed in clay."

Susan Peterson, *The Craft and Art of Clay*. Woodstock, NY: Overlook Press, 2000, p. 256.

A clay and ivory menorah created by Otto Natzler in 1977.

Germany and Austria to the United States. Marguerite Wildenhain (1896–1985) studied at the Bauhaus in Weimar, Germany, a school of design that merged the artist with the craftsperson and focused on functionality and beauty as well as the ability of the piece to be mass produced. Wildenhain achieved the level of master potter at the school, but after the Nazis gained power in Germany she was eventually asked to leave because she was Jewish. She came to the United States in 1939 and joined an artist community in northern California called Pond Farm.

Wildenhain ran the pottery school, taught students, sponsored workshops, and created her own distinctive pottery for more than forty years until her death. While in Europe, she created clean and sleek Bauhaus-type tableware, tea sets, and vases for mass production. Later, she produced pieces themed in nature, with plant and animal forms and carved figures and designs.

The husband and wife team of Gertrud and Otto Natzler (1908–1971; 1908–2007) fled Vienna, Austria, from the Nazis in 1938 and settled in Los Angeles in 1939. They worked as a team, but Gertrud produced the forms in one room, while Otto decorated them in another. Writer Suzanne Muchnic states, "[Gertrud] perfected her extraordinary talent for throwing paper-thin pots while [Otto] pursued his interest in chemistry by experimenting with glazes and developing more than 2,000 formulas for a wide variety of surface effects ranging from iridescent lusters to crystalline patterns to bubbly eruptions."[110]

The Natzlers created modern, simple forms with various textures and decorated them with vibrant reds, greens, and yellows. They mixed their own brick-red clay and during their collaboration from 1939 to 1971 produced over twenty-five thousand vessels. No figures were on their pottery, only glazes that ranged from glistening copper colors to flaming reds, streaked with black. Some textures were smooth, while others were pocked or pitted.

After World War II, potters in America started to develop a style of ceramics that contrasted with the techniques and methods of the past and promoted experimentation with clay. Abstract expressionism emerged, and Peter Voulkos (1924–2002) of Los Angeles, California, was the revolutionary potter who came to embody the new movement.

The Clay Revolution of Artistic Freedom

In a career that spanned fifty years, Voulkos moved from making conventional bowls and pots to monumental ceramic sculptures. The artist and potter Ken Price declared, "He is the most important person in clay of the 20th century."[111] Voulkos was first introduced to pottery when he took classes at Montana

SHE LIVED LIFE TO ITS FULLEST

The artist Beatrice Wood (1893–1998) was an eyewitness to nearly the entire twentieth century. She was born into a wealthy and privileged family and traveled the world. At first, Wood took up painting and drawing, but on a trip to Holland she bought a set of dessert plates that had a particularly beautiful luster glaze. When she could not find a matching teapot, she decided to make one herself and took a ceramics class at a local high school back in the United States. She became serious about pottery and eventually studied with Gertrud and Otto Natzler, who taught her about throwing and glazing. She made pots, bowls, and later, figurative sculpture. Her work was free and unconventional, and she produced luster glazes in exotic colors like green, gold, pink, and bronze. Some of Wood's most critically acclaimed work—tall luster-glazed chalices—was produced when she was in her nineties. She wrote several books, was married twice, and threw pottery on the wheel until she was 104 years old. The character of Rose in the movie *Titanic* was based partly on her remarkable life.

State College where he earned a bachelor's degree in 1951. He received a master of fine arts degree in ceramics from the California College of Arts and Crafts in Oakland in 1952. In 1954 he settled in Los Angeles as chairperson of the new Ceramics Department at what is now known as the Otis College of Art and Design. It was in Los Angeles in the 1950s that Voulkos turned the pottery world on its head. He moved away from conventionality and functionalism toward larger and larger expressive pieces.

Voulkos produced so many forms that he installed a giant bread dough mixer, which mixed powdered clay with water in enormous quantities. He worked with large mounds of clay that needed to be kept soft enough to work and mold. If the clay was too soft, the sculpture would collapse, but if the clay was too dry, it could become brittle and break. He used large humidifiers in his studio to control the moisture level in the room. Voulkos added clay slabs, cylinders, spheres, and disks to thrown pottery and built these forms on top of each other, developing a series of big sculptures about 3 to 5.5 feet (.91 to 1.52m) tall. All of his sculptures were painted with a black iron slip with a thin glaze wash. Many of the surfaces of his stoneware plates were slashed, gouged, pitted, and pock-marked.

A stoneware rocking pot created by American potter Peter Voulkos.

According to art historian Rose Slivka, "He used the wheel as the tool for spinning out the shapes he wanted and then combined them in complex and massive assemblage. . . . Together with ceramics engineer Mike Kalan they built . . . one of the largest updraft reduction kilns in a private studio at the time—120 cubic feet, six feet high by four feet deep [1.83 by 1.22m] with a five-foot-wide [1.52m] firing chamber"[112] to accommodate the larger pieces.

In the 1960s Voulkos worked at the University of California at Berkeley and settled in Oakland, California. He began to work in bronze, complet-

Historian Rose Slivka describes the artist's unique method of pottery production:

He will stack and join these [clay slabs and cylinders] in various combinations and sizes, or use them singly. These decisions he makes as he goes along, right on the spot, as he is making the piece. He does not plan or design in advance. He keeps his elements basic and achieves endless variety in form and surface within that simplicity. He is not a modeler or a carver. He is a thrower, and he limits his clay forms to those the wheel will spin and his hand or mallet can pound or press out. Voulkos once declared, "I don't like to use glazes. They cover up the detail. I like the clay to pick up on my fingerprints. I like to put my own marks on it." One Voulkos sculpture, *Gallas Rock*, was completed in 1960. It is 8 feet (2.44m) high and consists of more than one hundred wheel-thrown and slab pieces that are connected to an inner construction of cylinders that supports the weight of the clay slabs.

Rose Slivka, *Peter Voulkos: A Dialogue with Clay*. New York: New York Graphic Society in association with American Crafts Council, 1978, p. 102.

Quoted in Rose Slivka and Karen Tsujimoto, *The Art of Peter Voulkos*. New York and London: Kodansha International in collaboration with the Oakland Museum, 1995, p. 60.

ing an 18-foot-tall (5.49m) sculpture for an office lobby. He returned to clay in the late 1960s and by the late 1970s started to use an anagama, a Japanese wood-burning kiln. Voulkos loved the spontaneity of the anagama, in which temperatures were uneven and ash and soot often discolored his stacked pottery and plates of this period. Voulkos worked into the 1990s and continued to produce large clay pieces. A number of his students and contemporaries followed his lead in pottery and went on to pursue their own distinct and innovative careers.

Japanese Influences and Large and Small Ceramics

Paul Soldner (1922–) was Peter Voulkos's first graduate student, but he went a different direction with his clay. Soldner became interested in Japanese pottery and experimented with low-firing raku. In the 1960s Soldner used unglazed clay slabs with surface treatments pressed into the clay. In the 1970s and 1980s he worked with female figures as a vehicle for expressing contemporary themes. By the 1990s Soldner started to create more abstract pieces. "In my work, I use any technique I can think of," he stated, "smoke, manganese, wheel thrown, off wheel, slips and glazes, no slips and glazes, a welding torch—anything and everything."[113]

John Mason (1927–), also a Voulkos student, shared a studio with Voulkos in the 1950s. Early in his career Mason created large vertical sculptures and wall reliefs. Some were so large they had to be fired in pieces in oversize kilns, then assembled separately. Later, his work became more abstract and mathematical and included stacked firebricks in various geometric shapes and designs.

While many potters were making big clay sculptures, Ken Price (1935–) made what reporter Kristine McKenna describes as "small, discreet pieces infused with elegance, sensuality and wit. . . . He's turned out misshapen cups . . . weird hybrids combining industrial and organic shapes, and ominous eggs with maggot forms pushing through fissures in their shell."[114] Price used car paint for his multicolored glazes. He produced a series of 3- to 5-inch (7.62 to 12.7cm) architectural cups in bright colors, as well as his largest pieces—blob forms up to 23 inches (58.42cm) in height painted in bright blues and golds.

Japanese pottery like this black raku teabowl from the early seventeenth century interested Paul Soldner and led to his experimentation with the process of raku pottery.

Abstract Shapes, Huge Dumplings, and Ornate Vessels

The Montana potter and friend of Voulkos, Rudy Autio (1926–2007), once said, "There are always new possibilities in ceramics. You have to let them happen."[115] In the early part of his career, Autio used abstract patterns to decorate his pottery, then he began to paint nude male and female figures as well as horses and other animals on his ceramic surfaces. As the figures became more distinct, consisting of bucking horses and bent and distorted arms and legs, the shapes of the vessels became more obscure and larger in size.

Jun Kaneko (1942–) was once a student of Voulkos when he taught at UC Berkeley in the 1960s. Today, the Omaha-based Kaneko is known around the world for his large-scale abstract ceramic sculptures. His series of Dangos (which means "dumpling" in Japanese) are large, pillowy shapes. Some of these simple forms, decorated in bright colors in stripes, dots, spirals, or slashes, may weigh several tons and stand 8 to 13 feet (2.44 to 3.96m) tall. Depending on their size, up to four months of drying time can be required, and the firing process might last up to thirty-five days. Kaneko also produced glazed ceramic wall slabs of various designs and colors, and giant heads over 10 feet (3.05m) tall.

The focus of Adrian Saxe (1943–) has been his personal reinterpretation of eighteenth-century European porcelains. He creates classical and elegant ceramic forms, elaborately decorated with rich glazes and gold lusters. Then he adds Mickey Mouse ears, plastic action figures, fishing lures, or miniature animals. His pieces are both beautiful and outrageously witty. Saxe stated, "I use pottery as a . . . means to [question] what we consider art, how we value art in our society, and what the role of the decorative arts might be in our culture."[116]

California Funk, Superrealism, and Colossal Clay

Funk art was born out of abstract expressionism, and Robert Arneson (1930–1992) was considered the father of California

While West Coast potters were experimenting with form and expression in a variety of ways in the second half of the twentieth century, ceramicists in other parts of the nation continued to emphasize functional pottery and high-fired stoneware and porcelain.

Robert Turner (1913–2004) worked mainly in New York. He first focused on utilitarian pieces, then became inspired by visits to the American Southwest, Italy, and Africa. He was captivated by the unpredictability of the clay and once said, "I look forward to accidents because they reveal the way things work. They reveal natural events." The legacy of Ken Ferguson (1928–2004) in ceramics was as an exceptional teacher at the Kansas City Art Institute in Missouri. According to authors Lorenzo Camusso and Sandro Bortone, he "encourage[d] his students to achieve . . . honesty of purpose and materials while . . . directing them to peruse the ceramics of other times and cultures for inspiration and technical knowledge." The work of Akio Takamori (1950–) a student of Ferguson, consists of large decorated pots, sculptures based on the human body, and most recently, multiple-figured pieces. The use of black lines in his work is similar to Japanese wood prints. Takamori currently lives and works in Seattle, Washington.

Kurt Weiser (1950–) of Tempe, Arizona, another student of Ferguson, creates porcelain jars, teapots, and other vessels with detailed china-painted decorations requiring multiple firings. His pieces are noted for their bright colors and lush landscapes and scenery. The porcelain pots of Pittsburgh, Pennsylvania, ceramicist Edward Eberle (1944–) resemble Greek vases. Art critic Kurt Shaw writes that his pots "are embellished with black-and-white paintings of figures that he creates with a technique known as terra sigillata, which produces a very smooth coating of clay that resembles a glaze and is virtually waterproof."

Quoted in Jimmy Clark, "Robert Turner," *American Craft*, October/November 2002, p. 62.

Lorenzo Camusso and Sandro Bortone, *Ceramics of the World from 4,000 B.C. to the Present*. New York: Harry N. Abrams, 1991, p. 269.

Kurt Shaw, "Concept Art Gallery Exhibit Highlights Pittsburgh's Edward Eberle," *Pittsburgh Tribune-Review*, May 10, 2007.

Funk. Cooper describes the movement as "outrageous, even disgusting, it . . . challenged concepts of 'correct' or 'incorrect' and what was a 'legitimate' use for clay."[117] The ceramics of Arneson often focused on personal subjects—his opposition to war and the military, humorous self-portraits, and tributes in clay to other artists. Arneson used ordinary objects or well-known personalities in many of his pieces. Fingers extend out of a toaster in *Toasties*. The keys on his work *Typewriter* are red-painted fingernails. The head and shoulders of a greenish George Washington (as he appears on the dollar bill) beams at the head and shoulders of a smiling Mona Lisa in the aptly titled *George and Mona in the Baths of Coloma*.

In response to the outrageousness of funk came the superrealism of Marilyn Levine (1935–) and the larger-than-life figures of Viola Frey (1933–2004). Levine's stoneware sculptures of suitcases, purses, and other leather items are so real-looking that, as Cooper explains, "Only through touch can the 'unreal' nature of the objects become apparent and convey the idea that things may not be what they seem."[118] Frey is best known for her colossal clay figures of men and women, some of which are 10 to 11 feet (3.05 to 3.35m) tall. Ranging from business people to housewives in floral dresses, Frey's figures are brightly colored, with various expressions.

The studio potters who emerged in the twentieth century all contributed to the variety of techniques and diverse styles used by present-day potters to create meaningful works of art.

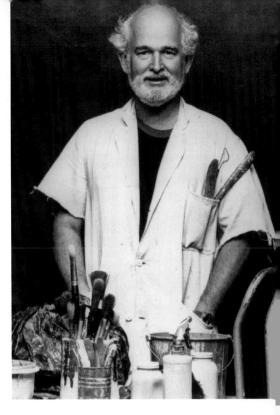

American ceramist and father of California Funk art Robert Arneson often used ordinary objects and well-known people in his artwork.

7

Contemporary Potters—a Diversity of Style

Clay is the only art material that changes, that never stays the same until after the final firing, that evokes different emotions at different stages, that does not reveal itself until the final cooling.

—Susan Peterson, *The Craft and Art of Clay*

Present-day potters have the artistic freedom to create works of art using any style and developing any technique, both functional and nonfunctional. Some have expressed personal emotions and opinions, others have reproduced processes and forms in nature, and still others have revived and/or reinvented ceramic traditions of the past. Contemporary pottery encompasses many individuals and a variety of methods that all have a common connection—the choice, delight, and satisfaction of working with clay.

Elegant Minimalist Forms

The Dutch artist Geert Lap (1951–) is a minimalist potter, whose work is reduced to its most fundamental form, devoid of surface decoration, glazes, and other ornamentation. He uses the traditional wheel and handmade methods to create vases and bowls of stoneware, but he is not concerned with their functionality.

For Lap, it is all about form and color, elegance and perfection. His vessels are smooth from every angle but sharply defined at the shoulders, rim or lip. The surfaces are dull, not shiny. Before firing, one color is applied to the surface with pigmented slip.

Koplos describes Lap's vessels: "Their contours are so liquid, so continuous, that one's eyes are continually drawn around the forms. . . . Often these vessels create an impression of motion, as if for an instant one could see backward in time to the softness of the clay as it whirled on the wheel under the pressure of the artist's hands."[119]

Pattern and Decoration

In the past, decorative ceramics was not considered serious art. With the Pattern and Decoration movement of the 1970s, what is called P and D acquired new legitimacy. Betty Woodman (1930–) is closely identified with this movement. In the early part of her career she produced traditional functional pottery and became known for her Pillow Pitchers, which were large round-bottom pots.

Over time her focus changed. "Function has become less important in my work," she states, "but has remained an important symbolic factor. I don't want to obliterate the line between pottery and sculpture."[120] Vessels are still a central part of her work. She has hung them on walls and experimented with glazing and multicolored surfaces. Some consider Woodman a painter as well as a ceramicist and sculptor. Writer Barry Schwabsky asserts that "pottery is a subject of her art as well as its primary medium. Even the flat elements in her pieces tell us by their swirling surfaces that they've been formed on the wheel."[121]

Woodman decorates her surfaces with bright and bold colors in various patterns. Her vases and pots stand alone or are wall mounted in segments with spaces in between. They can be flat or outlined, sit on a shelf or have handles, and are multiglazed and lacquer painted. Schwabsky declares that Woodman "is using her clay to sculpt the air in and around . . . the very atmosphere of the place it inhabits. . . . She does everything she can with color and shape to lend clay airy qualities of its very own."[122]

REVIVAL OF NATIVE CERAMIC TRADITIONS

*L*ucy M. Lewis (ca. 1898–1992) was a Pueblo Indian potter who lived her life in Acoma, New Mexico, "the oldest continuously inhabited settlement in North America." Artist and educator Susan Peterson writes that Lewis "found old fine-lined black-on-white [Anasazi] Mimbres motifs on shards. . . . Her pueblo . . . was no longer working in the older tradition, but Lewis revived it, painting highly stylized geometric black designs onto burnished white clay, using the chewed end of a yucca frond as a brush with which to make fine, precise lines."

Lewis learned to make pottery as a young girl by watching other women. She dug up and prepared her own clay and used the coil method of production. After smoothing the surface with tools made from gourds, she covered it with a white slip, painted the designs, and fired the pots in a handmade outdoor kiln.

Lewis taught pottery making and firing at the Idyllwild School of Music and the Arts in California for many years and traveled around the country leading pottery workshops. She won many awards and her pots are exhibited in museums around the world.

New York Times, "Lucy M. Lewis Dies; Self-Taught Potter, 93," March 26, 1992. www.nytimes.com.

Susan Peterson, *The Craft and Art of Clay*. Woodstock, NY: Overlook Press, 2000, p. 279.

Abstract Versions of Functional Industrial Forms

Marek Cecula (1944–) creates porcelain pieces that look like they have a specific purpose but are actually abstract interpretations. His works from the 1990s look like containers you might find in a hospital. In 1996 an exhibition called Hygiene consisted of objects made of china, wood, and steel used for washing and body waste. Cecula removed these objects from their functional context into the realm of art, while also referring to what reviewer Roberta Lord calls "the public-health consequences of careless hygiene."[123]

In his more recent work, he subjected his ceramic pieces to a wood-fired Japanese anagama kiln to purposely create imperfections and deformities. In a 2007 exhibit called The Beauty of Imperfection, he continued this idea by using air, fire, and water to break down and change the form, function, and attractiveness of the porcelain pieces.

In *The Stand*, Cecula created a full-size Olympic Games awards platform made from white porcelain slabs that would collapse in a heap if any weight was applied. Cecula states, "It's a symbol of a hierarchy . . . that can't support itself."[124] Lord writes, "It is strong commentary on the myth of status in the art world."[125] In *The Porcelain Carpet*, Cecula shows three stages in the production of a 12-by-16-inch (30.48-by-40.64cm) oriental rug laid over 10¼-inch (26.04cm) porcelain dinner plates. This is another instance in which weight cannot be applied and the carpet cannot be walked on. According to Lord, "The clay is presented as multiples of an industrial, standardized product—in this case, the dinner plate—onto which the 'art' is literally overlaid. . . . Carpets and ceramics are both hand and mechanically produced, both require skilled craftsmanship, and both are simultaneously decorative and utilitarian."[126]

Roxanne Swentzell's bronze figures, such as *Window to the Past,* deal with a wide range of human emotions.

Sculptor of Human Emotions

As a young girl with a serious speech problem, the only way Roxanne Swentzell (1963–) communicated with people was by making small clay figures. The faces on the figures revealed her feelings. "Art became her lifeline,"[127] declares writer Dottie Indyke. Born into a family of potters in New Mexico, she learned the traditional hand-coiled method by watching her mother, who was also a potter.

Her works deal with a wide range of human emotions, from self-image to loss of cultural identity to connecting with the past. Her clay figures express anger, love, and sadness, and in 1997 Swentzell began to cast them in bronze. Indyke wrote, "Each figure embodies a spark of life as unique as any human being, imbued by the artist as she coils and shapes her clay. It's a process that can't be forced."[128]

In *Despairing Clown*, Swentzell explains that "he's peeling off his stripes to see what's underneath. . . . We all need to examine what's beneath the surface. . . . Our masks can sometimes become a prison in which we forget who we really are inside."[129] The female clay figure in *In Crisis* is grabbing a hand with red nails and keeping it away. According to Swentzell, "She recognizes that these images of what she's supposed to be, especially from television, are an attack on her."[130] An expressionless porcelain doll's face covers the face of a clay figure, hiding her emotions in *Hidden Feelings*. "When you take the mask away," states Swentzell, "she looks vulnerable and frightened."[131] The messages and emotions of her figures reach out and connect with all people.

Older soup tureens, like this one from 1730 with ram-head handles, have become influential pieces for ceramicist David Regan.

Humor in Pottery

Ceramicist David Regan (1964–) covers his elaborate forms in black slip and carves through the surface to reveal the white porcelain underneath. This is the technique of sgraffito, which Regan has created both humorous and serious vases, teapots, and other vessels. His 2003 piece titled *Ark* consists of animals climbing out of a pop-up book and crowding into a NASA rocket-powered vehicle.

What really fascinates Regan is soup tureens. Through his studies of eighteenth-century European bowls, he became interested in what writer Jo Lauria describes as "their ample, buoyant forms and exuberant surface flourishes of elaborate texture, color

SMALL, WHIMSICAL PORCELAIN THAT SWELLS AND FOLDS

It is easy to see the influence of California Funk artist Robert Arneson in the work of Kathy Butterly (1963–). Butterly studied with Arneson and makes porcelain cuplike vessels 3 to 8 inches (7.62 to 20.32cm) tall, with various attachments and embellishments, that sit on ceramic bases in a mixture of styles, both past and present. Her vessels are brightly colored with multiple layers of glaze.

Words like bizarre, grotesque, and irreverent, as well as humorous, touching, and vulnerable, have been used to describe her work. Art critic Christopher Miles writes that Butterly's pieces "seem to be trying to hold it together. Although made of enduring materials, her small pieces suggest the stability of a soufflé, a house loose on its foundation or someone trying to walk on heels for the first time."

"Ms. Butterly begins the process of making each piece by hollowing traditional cup and vase forms in wet clay," explains reviewer Benjamin Genocchio. "She then prods, nudges and pulls these forms until they slump, fold or collapse in an agreeably curvaceous way. . . . She refines them with the addition of whimsical ornamental details—odd appendages, zany webbed lids, coral-like interiors, and even ropes of little pearly beads."

Christopher Miles, "Art; Around the Galleries; Ceramics: Such Fragile Objects," *Los Angeles Times*, November 11, 2005, p. E28.

Benjamin Genocchio, "Quirky and Textured, Works Vie for Attention," *New York Times*, November 6, 2005, p. 14WC.8.

and gilding."[132] Regan was also enthralled with how certain tureens were decorated to reflect what was inside. Lauria writes, "The main ingredient of the stew or pottage was announced in the shape of the container."[133] Regan creates tureens in vegetable and animal shapes.

Taking it a step further, Regan's soup tureens sometimes communicate more than the viewer (or eater) bargained for. In *Fish Tureen* a large fish swallowing another smaller one is caught in the net of a fisherman. In *Deer Tureen* a fawn emerging from its mother's womb confronts a hungry snake. In *Snake Tureen* the serpent has obviously swallowed a person whole by the looks of its proportionately swollen body. Not all of Regan's pieces are dark. A borscht tureen illustrates the ingredients and preparation of this Russian soup and includes a peasant woman in a chair surrounded by beets and cabbage.

Geological Processes in Porcelain

The titles of artist Paula Winokur's pieces are self-explanatory, like this work titled *Global Warnings*. The piece contains fifty-five porcelain globes, all of which are cracked or distorted.

Ceramic artist Paula Winokur (1935–) focuses on the landscape and geological developments in nature from a variety of views. Her early pieces were functional vessels in stoneware, but since the 1970s she has worked only in porcelain. "It comes from the earth as pure white, strong and durable," says Winokur, "[and] . . . has allowed me to explore issues in the landscape without necessarily making literal interpretations."[134] Winokur has produced porcelain box forms and thin porcelain bowls balanced on porcelain ledges. Since the early 1980s, her work has focused on larger sculptural pieces that stand alone,

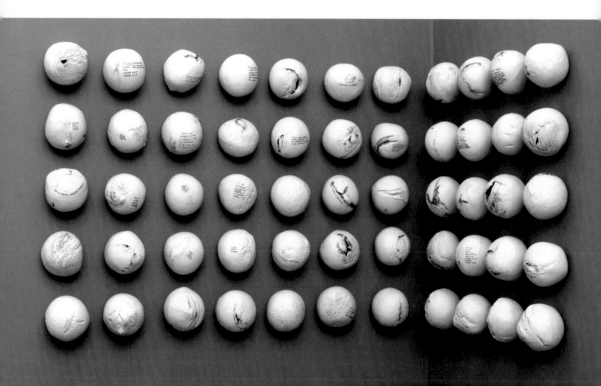

STILL LIFE TO TEXTURAL FORMS

The ceramic artwork of Andrew Lord (1950–) has focused on recreating the still life process in painting and the effect of light on the pieces. He groups his tall hand-built vases, jars, cups, pitchers, and jugs in clusters (mostly in twos and threes, but sometimes more) on low or high platforms. Reviewer Janet Koplos writes, "Lord's clay is usually rough-surfaced; his objects are essentially traditional in format but often distorted and oversize . . . [they] are uniformly covered with a pale monochrome glaze."

Twelve Mexican Pieces is an assemblage of various oversize vessels, including a three-legged round pot, a small table with three very thin legs, and various jugs, pitchers, and vases with a mixture of handles— vertical, twisted, small, and supersize. Koplos describes the surface of the vessels as "finger-scraped texture."

A piece titled *Breathing* is depicted by reviewer Roberta Smith as "slightly billowing . . . [that] suggest someone blowing from the inside." *Swallowing* consists of two vessels with thick and lumpy bulges, indicating the ingestion of food. *Biting* has Lord's teeth marks all over it. According to Smith, the pieces titled *Listening, Watching,* and *Smelling* "have been formed by repeated applications of the artist's . . . nose, eyes or ears." Over time, the vessels of Andrew Lord have moved from the classical forms of still life painting to more instinctive physical and textural forms.

Janet Koplos, "Not-So-Still Life," *Art in America*, April 2005, p. 134.

Roberta Smith, "Andrew Lord," *New York Times*, September 17, 2004, p. E.2:32.

on a base, or are wall mounted. *Mantel for Three Bowls* is a series of porcelain wall ledges attached to vertical pieces that seem to indicate a rocky, desert landscape.

Winokur creates her sculpture in sections using slabs of clay, which are connected together. Many of the surfaces are seen in an aerial view, looking down on plains, rocks, glaciers, and other landscapes. The titles of her pieces are self-explanatory— *Shattered Ice, Ice Cones, Glacier Ledge, Boulder Field,* and *Canyon Slice,* which is 84 inches (2.13m) tall. A corner installation called *Global Warnings* consists of fifty-five 5-inch (12.7cm) porcelain globes, all of which are cracked or distorted in some way.

Winokur describes her ceramic response to the natural environment: "The earth itself, particularly cliffs, ledges, crevices and canyons: the effects of wind, earthquakes, glaciers and other natural phenomena such as geological 'shifts' and 'faults' interest me." She also focuses on "the many ways man has marked and scarred the land."[135]

Yixing: Traditional Chinese Pottery

Luo Xiaoping (1960–) spends half of the year at his studio in Yixing (pronounced *ee-shing*) in China's Jiangsu Province and the other half in Arizona. Xiaoping refers to Yixing as "the sacred place of pottery."[136] Teapots made from this area's unique purple clay called zisha have been produced since the Sung dynasty (A.D. 960–1280). These unglazed pots are very porous when fired, so they absorb the flavor of the tea and keep it hot.

Xiaoping used the special clay at Yixing to create various sculptures, but his teapots, according to reviewer Kathleen Vanesian, are "often enormous in scale," and more "fantastic" than functional.[137] He also produces large single figures from zisha, which were purposely fired at high temperatures, resulting in cracks and imperfections of the clay.

Xiaoping's most well-known sculpture is *Time Square Series* in which he created from purple clay and stoneware more than twenty 2-foot-high (.61m) clay figures of the most powerful and well-known people in the world. From George W. Bush to Osama bin Laden to Fidel Castro to Kim Jong Il, these very recognizable figures all stand together in goofy poses and assorted hand gestures. Vanesian writes, "Each leader wears an identical Tang-style jacket with mandarin collar, stamped with traditional Chinese characters representing luck, fortune, longevity and happiness."[138]

Seventeenth- and Eighteenth- Century English Ceramics

The British pottery tradition is the basis of most of the work of American Michelle Erickson (1961–) Through research and experimentation, she has reproduced a wide array of ceramics and glazes in the English tradition—from handmade medieval pottery to soft-paste porcelains to Jasperware by Wedgwood. She has applied these same methods to her own original artwork. Erickson states, "The evolution of these rich and varied ceramic techniques permeates my works . . . and provides a unique glimpse into the past through the present."

Teapot Towers are her signature pieces in which historical forms are positioned one on top of each other. In a single sculpture, Erickson intermingles several historical techniques and styles. *Black Teapot with Blue Bird, 2001*, according to writer Glenn Adamson, is "a meditation on the fragility and haphazardness of old ceramics." The main body of the teapot is based on English stoneware methods of the seventeenth century, while a variety of Chinese techniques make up the spout and handle.

Adamson writes, "Atop the teapot is an absurdly overgrown version of the bird finials that sometimes served as the handles for teapot lids, and underneath is a stand, featuring a simulation of a tea egg that has hatched two spindly legs. The legs in turn appear to wobble on an overturned blue and white porcelain cup, complete with a spill of tea-colored glaze." He declares, "It seems as if the stack of forms might come crashing down at any moment." Erickson states, "The imagery embodied in my pots tends to reflect the underlying archetypes of the human condition regardless of time period or cultural beliefs."

Michelle Erickson, "ME Michelle Erickson." www.perioddesigns.com/Michelle%20Erickson.html.

Glenn Adamson, "Michelle Erickson," *American Craft*, August/September 2002, p. 56.

Concerned about war and violence in the world, Xiaoping declares, "They stand ready to negotiate. They may never be able to agree with each other, and that is acceptable, as long as they can put down their weapons and begin talking. We may never know their true thoughts, but it does not matter. All we are looking for is a life of peace and sweet dreams."[139]

Closed Forms of Stoneware and Porcelain

Toshiko Takaezu (1922–) has evolved from making functional ceramic pieces, such as teapots, to sculptural works that involve a variety of vivid glazes and painting. Her fifty-year career has resulted in clay creations of every shape and size, but her three-dimensional painted closed forms became her signature pieces. Writer Carol Strickland states, "She found her own identity as an artist when she sealed her pots. . . . The pieces vary, from forms resembling human hearts and torsos to ovoid or cylindrical closed forms and round, boulder-like spheres she calls 'moons.'"[140]

Takaezu has likened the application of glaze to her pieces as musical movement. "I like the idea of going around the piece and glazing—it's almost like dancing. You want the combination of form and glaze to fit. . . . I take a little bit of cobalt and iron, mix it up and put it on. But it's also the way you apply the cobalt, how thick or thin, how dry the brush is and what else you've added . . . to make it different."[141]

Nature is an important part of her work and a guiding force. According to reviewer Benjamin Genocchio, Takaezu finishes her pieces with "mostly earth-toned glazes that variously evoke bamboo, the ocean, sunsets, fluttering leaves, tall grasses, storm clouds moving across the sky and other natural phenomena."[142] One of her major pieces, *Tree-Man Forest*, consists of 7-foot-tall (2.13m) treelike sculptures inspired by an area in Hawaii called Devastation Forest in which lava flows from local volcanoes has destroyed all tree growth.

In past work, Takaezu dropped a clay bead inside her forms before closing them to give the piece the added element of

Toshiko Takaezu attaches a musical quality to the process of the glazing of her works such as this stoneware piece titled *Full Moon*.

sound. Her most recent work is a series of vessels with creases across the top. Genocchio compares them to "ripe peaches" and writes, "Sometimes the cuts are so deep that they open up a slit in the vessel, allowing you to look inside."[143] Takaezu admits, "I don't follow the rules. . . . Let the clay speak for itself and keep it alive. . . . Everything I make, you don't know why or how I make it or what it represents, because I really don't know. . . . What I don't know is what pushes me to work."[144]

Since ancient times, pottery has been characterized and examined in terms of its functional use and in relation to cultural styles and production methods. Contemporary pottery has evolved from utilitarian purposes to a diversity of artistic expression, limited only by the imagination and creativity of the individual potter.

Notes

Introduction: The Origins of Pottery

1. Prudence M. Rice, *Pottery Analysis*. Chicago: University of Chicago Press, 1987, p. 8.
2. William K. Barnett and John W. Hoopes, *The Emergence of Pottery*. Washington, DC: Smithsonian Institution Press, 1995, pp. 2, 4.
3. Quoted in Barnett and Hoopes, *The Emergence of Pottery*, p. 278.
4. Quoted in Sander E. van der Leeuw and Robin Torrence, eds., *What's New? A Closer Look at the Process of Innovation*. London: Unwin Hyman, 1989, pp. 215–16.
5. Rice, *Pottery Analysis*, p. 439.
6. Rice, *Pottery Analysis*, pp. 439–40.
7. Rice, *Pottery Analysis*, p. 441.

Chapter 1: Pottery Basics

8. Rice, *Pottery Analysis*, p. 8.
9. Glenn C. Nelson and Richard Burkett, *Ceramics: A Potter's Handbook*. Fort Worth, TX: Harcourt Brace, 1988, p. 129.
10. Nelson and Burkett, *Ceramics: A Potter's Handbook*, p. 165.
11. Emmanuel Cooper, *A History of World Pottery*. Radnor, PA: Chilton, 1991, p. 15.

12. Susan Peterson, *The Craft and Art of Clay*. Woodstock, NY: Overlook Press, 2000, p. 50.
13. Rice, *Pottery Analysis*, p. 134.
14. Rice, *Pottery Analysis*, p. 135.
15. Nelson and Burkett, *Ceramics: A Potter's Handbook*, p. 181.
16. Dora M. Billington, *The Technique of Pottery*. New York: Hearthside, 1962, p. 155.
17. Peterson, *The Craft and Art of Clay*, p. 134.
18. Rice, *Pottery Analysis*, p. 5.
19. Rice, *Pottery Analysis*, p. 6.
20. Peterson, *The Craft and Art of Clay*, p. 205.

Chapter 2: East Asia

21. Quoted in Barnett and Hoopes, *The Emergence of Pottery*, p. 14.
22. Quoted in Barnett and Hoopes, *The Emergence of Pottery*, p. 15.
23. Nelson and Burkett, *Ceramics: A Potter's Handbook*, p. 25.
24. Cooper, *A History of World Pottery*, p. 59.
25. Robert J. Charleston, ed., *World Ceramics*, Secaucus, NJ: Chartwell Books, p. 66.
26. Lorenzo Camusso and Sandro Bortone, eds., *Ceramics of the World from 4,000*

B.C. to the Present. New York: Harry N. Abrams, 1991, p. 368.

27. Polly Rothenberg, *The Complete Book of Ceramic Art*. New York: Crown, 1972, pp. 219–20.
28. Cooper, *A History of World Pottery*, p. 47.
29. Cooper, *A History of World Pottery*, p. 48.
30. Camusso and Bortone, *Ceramics of the World*, p. 289.
31. Rice, *Pottery Analysis*, p.16.
32. Quoted in David W. Richerson, *The Magic of Ceramics*. Westerville, OH: American Ceramic Society, 2000, p. 23.
33. Cooper, *A History of World Pottery*, p. 50.
34. Charleston, *World Ceramics*, p. 52.
35. Rice, *Pottery Analysis*, p. 17.
36. Richerson, *The Magic of Ceramics*, p. 44.
37. Cooper, *A History of World Pottery*, p. 57.
38. Charleston, *World Ceramics*, p. 63.

Chapter 3: The Near and Middle East

39. Nelson and Burkett, *Ceramics: A Potter's Handbook*, p. 35.
40. Quoted in Barnett and Hoopes, *The Emergence of Pottery*, p. 40.
41. Rice, *Pottery Analysis*, p. 10.
42. Peterson, *The Craft and Art of Clay*, p. 69.
43. Charleston, *World Ceramics*, p. 24.
44. Nelson and Burkett, *Ceramics: A Potter's Handbook*, p. 36.
45. Cooper, *A History of World Pottery*, p. 21.
46. Charleston, *World Ceramics*, p. 26.
47. Cooper, *A History of World Pottery*, p. 64.
48. Cooper, *A History of World Pottery*, p. 66.
49. Nelson and Burkett, *Ceramics: A Potter's Handbook*, p. 60.
50. Charleston, *World Ceramics*, p. 70.
51. Cooper, *A History of World Pottery*, p. 64.
52. Cooper, *A History of World Pottery*, p. 67.
53. Charleston, *World Ceramics*, p. 75.
54. Charleston, *World Ceramics*, p. 75.
55. Cooper, *A History of World Pottery*, p. 71.
56. Charleston, *World Ceramics*, p. 75.
57. Camusso and Bortone, *Ceramics of the World*, p. 105.
58. Cooper, *A History of World Pottery*, p. 76.
59. Nelson and Burkett, *Ceramics: A Potter's Handbook*, p. 62
60. Cooper, *A History of World Pottery*, p. 73.
61. Nelson and Burkett, *Ceramics: A Potter's Handbook*, p. 62.
62. Cooper, *A History of World Pottery*, p. 73.
63. Cooper, *A History of World Pottery*, p. 77.
64. Cooper, *A History of World Pottery*, p. 77.
65. Cooper, *A History of World Pottery*, p. 78.
66. Charleston, *World Ceramics*, p. 97.

Chapter 4: Europe

67. Nelson and Burkett, *Ceramics: A Potter's Handbook*, p. 42.
68. Charleston, *World Ceramics*, p. 33.

69. Cooper, *A History of World Pottery*, p. 38.
70. Cooper, *A History of World Pottery*, p. 86.
71. Rice, *Pottery Analysis*, p. 19.
72. Cooper, *A History of World Pottery*, p. 95.
73. Charleston, *World Ceramics*, p. 120.
74. Charleston, *World Ceramics*, p. 185.
75. Charleston, *World Ceramics*, p. 215.
76. Charleston, *World Ceramics*, p. 238.
77. Cooper, *A History of World Pottery*, pp. 101–2.
78. Cooper, *A History of World Pottery*, p. 105.
79. Cooper, *A History of World Pottery*, p. 106.
80. Cooper, *A History of World Pottery*, p. 116.
81. Nelson and Burkett, *Ceramics: A Potter's Handbook*, p. 72.
82. Charleston, *World Ceramics*, p. 123.
83. Cooper, *A History of World Pottery*, p. 118.
84. Charleston, *World Ceramics*, p. 268.
85. Peterson, *The Craft and Art of Clay*, p. 254.
86. Nelson and Burkett, *Ceramics: A Potter's Handbook*, p. 77.

Chapter 5: The Americas

87. Cooper, *A History of World Pottery*, p. 138.
88. Charleston, *World Ceramics*, p. 329.
89. Nelson and Burkett, *Ceramics: A Potter's Handbook*, p. 27.
90. Nelson and Burkett, *Ceramics: A Potter's Handbook*, p. 28.
91. Charleston, *World Ceramics*, p. 330.
92. Rice, *Pottery Analysis*, p. 21.
93. Cooper, *A History of World Pottery*, p. 145.
94. Cooper, *A History of World Pottery*, p. 147.
95. Charleston, *World Ceramics*, p. 332.
96. Nelson and Burkett, *Ceramics: A Potter's Handbook*, p. 33.
97. Charleston, *World Ceramics*, p. 333.
98. Cooper, *A History of World Pottery*, p. 140.
99. Charleston, *World Ceramics*, p. 328.
100. Rice, *Pottery Analysis*, pp. 21–22.
101. Harold F. Guilland, *Early American Folk Pottery*. Philadelphia: Chilton, 1971, p. 28.
102. Guilland, *Early American Folk Pottery*, p. 34.
103. Guilland, *Early American Folk Pottery*, p. 35.
104. Guilland, *Early American Folk Pottery*, p. 56.
105. Camusso and Bortone, *Ceramics of the World*, p. 266.
106. Charleston, *World Ceramics*, p. 313.

Chapter 6: The Emergence of Studio Potters

107. Cooper, *A History of World Pottery*, pp. 178–79.
108. Janet Koplos, "Review of Exhibitions: Lucie Rie & Hans Coper at the Metropolitan Museum," *Art in America*, April 1995, p. 111.
109. Koplos, "Review of Exhibitions," p. 111.
110. Suzanne Muchnic, "Art & Architecture; A Remarkable Alliance of Form; Otto Natzler Recalls the Days When He and His Late Wife, Gertrud, Used His Glazes to Bring Life to Her Simple-Shaped Pottery," *Los Angeles Times*, May 14, 2000, p. 59.

111. Quoted in Hunter Drohojowska-Philp, "Arts & Architecture; Breaking Ground Still Fires Him Up; in the 50s, Peter Voulkos Rewrote the Rules of Ceramics. At 75, He Maintains That Energy with His Teaching and Works," *Los Angeles Times*, November 14, 1999, p. 62.

112. Rose Slivka, *Peter Voulkos: A Dialogue with Clay*. New York: New York Graphic Society in association with American Crafts Council, 1978, p. 39.

113. Quoted in Peterson, *The Craft and Art of Clay*, p. 318.

114. Kristine McKenna, "Reshaping the Image of Clay; Ken Price, a Part of a 50s Mutinous Gang That Yanked the Material Out of the World of Demure Teapots and into the Avant Garde, Is the Subject of an Exhibition," *Los Angeles Times*, January 7, 1996, p. 63.

115. Quoted in Peterson, *The Craft and Art of Clay*, p. 286.

116. Quoted in Peterson, *The Craft and Art of Clay*, p. 316.

117. Cooper, *A History of World Pottery*, p. 189.

118. Cooper, *A History of World Pottery*, p. 190.

Chapter 7: Contemporary Potters—a Diversity of Style

119. Janet Koplos, "Geert Lap at Garth Clark—Ceramics Exhibition; New York, New York," *Art in America*, September 1993.

120. Quoted in Peterson, *The Craft and Art of Clay*, p. 328.

121. Barry Schwabsky, "The Pot *Is* Betty Woodman's Central Idea," *American Craft*, April/May 2000, p. 64.

122. Schwabsky, "The Pot *Is* Betty Woodman's Central Idea," p. 64.

123. Roberta Lord, "Marek Cecula, the Porcelain Carpet Project," *Grand Arts*, January 5/March 16, 2002, www.grandarts.com/exhibits/MCecula.html.

124. Quoted in Lord, "Marek Cecula."

125. Lord, "Marek Cecula."

126. Lord, "Marek Cecula."

127. Dottie Indyke, "Roxanne Swentzell," *Southwest Art*, August 2001, p. 190.

128. Indyke, "Roxanne Swentzell," p. 190.

129. Quoted in Alicia Herrin, "Roxanne Swentzell: Extraordinary People," *Southwest Art*, August 2002, p. 228.

130. Quoted in Herrin, "Roxanne Swentzell: Extraordinary People," p. 228.

131. Quoted in Herrin, "Roxanne Swentzell: Extraordinary People," p. 228.

132. Jo Lauria, "David Regan: Tureen Terrain," *American Craft*, December 1998/January 1999, p. 46.

133. Lauria, "David Regan," p. 46.

134. Paula Winokur, "Artist Statement." www.paulawinokur.com/as.html.

135. Winokur, "Artist Statement."

136. Quoted in Kathleen Vanesian, "Luo Xiaoping," *American Craft*, April/May 2004, p. 72.

137. Vanesian, "Luo Xiaoping," p. 72.

138. Vanesian, "Luo Xiaoping," p. 72.

139. Quoted in Arizona State University Art Museum, "Luo Xiaoping: Time Square Series," p. 2. asuartmuseum.asu.edu/forms/timesquare-gg.pdf.

140. Carol Strickland, "Master of Art and the Art of Living, Everything

Ceramic Artist Toshiko Takaezu Does Feeds into the Process of Discovering and Creating, *Christian Science Monitor*, October 6, 1997, p. 10.

141. Quoted in Althea Meade-Hajduk, "A Talk with Toshiko Takaezu, *American Craft*, February/March 2005, p. 46.

142. Benjamin Genocchio, "Master Who Turns Mud into Vessels of Beauty," *New York Times*, July 23, 2006, p. 14NJ.14.

143. Genocchio, "Master Who Turns Mud into Vessels of Beauty," p. 14NJ.14.

144. Quoted in Meade-Hajduk, "A Talk with Toshiko Takaezu," p. 46.

Glossary

abrade: To scrape, rub, or wear down the surface.

abstract: Nonrepresentational expressions of forms or objects.

aesthetic: A sense of beauty.

alkali: Any of various bases that neutralize acids.

anagama: Japanese tubelike kiln built in the slope of a hill.

arabesque: Interwoven line design that forms flowers and foliage.

archetype: Original pattern or model.

biscuit-fired: Unglazed, fired only once.

bladder: A sac in which liquid is stored.

burnish: Polish to make shiny.

celadon: A range of mainly sea green to dark green glazes (with a hint of blue or gray) used on stoneware or porcelain.

dung: Animal waste.

englobe: Liquid clay slip coating of various colors.

finial: Ornamental projection.

firebrick: Clay in the shape of bricks that can withstand high temperatures.

frit: Melted and fired mixture that is ground to a powder and used in glazes.

funerary: Associated with burials and funerals.

galena: A powdered form of lead that produces a lead glaze on clay when fired.

glaze: The smooth glossy surface or coating on ceramics.

harlequin: Comic character.

incising: Carving or engraving on a clay surface.

iridescent: The appearance of changing colors like a rainbow.

irreverent: Disrespectful, impudent.

kiln: A heated enclosure, furnace, or oven for firing clay.

lattice: Mesh, netting.

luster: Iridescent, metallic glaze.

maize: Types of corn.

malleable: Flexible, easily shaped.

minimalist: Reduced to its most fundamental form, without decoration.

monochrome: Single color.

mosque: Islamic place of worship.

motif: Central theme or main idea.

naturalistic: Imitating forms in nature.

opaque: Dull and cloudy, not allowing light to pass through.

oxidizing atmosphere: Unlimited oxygen within a kiln.

permeable: Tiny holes or openings that allow liquid to leak through. See **porous**.

polychrome: Several colors.

porous: Able to be penetrated by fluids. See **permeable**.

raku: A form of quick firing associated with tea wares in Japan.

reducing atmosphere: Limited oxygen within a kiln, causing it to become smoky.

relief: Raised surface or projection.

secular: Nonreligious.

sgraffito: Decoration scratched or cut through slip or glaze to reveal the background color.

shard: Broken fragment of pottery.

stamping: A distinct mark on the clay surface made when pressing or imprinting.

stylized: Distinct characteristics that represent a specific form or design.

symmetrical: Proportional, balanced.

synthetic: Produced artificially, not genuine.

terra sigillata: Red-slip earthenware associated with Roman pottery; slip glaze that shines when fired at low temperatures.

translucent: Allows light to pass through but is not transparent.

utilitarian: Useful and practical.

vitrification: The process in which materials fuse together at a certain temperature and change into a glassy substance.

vulnerable: Open, susceptible.

For Further Reading

Books

Tony Birks, *The Complete Potter's Companion*. Boston: Little, Brown, 1998. Readable, well-illustrated overview of all phases of pottery making.

Garth Clark, *The Artful Teapot*. New York: Watson-Guptill, 2001. Focuses on the teapot as a form of artistic expression through five centuries. Excellent illustrations.

Mark Del Vecchio, *Postmodern Ceramics*. New York: Thames & Hudson, 2001. Beautifully illustrated international collection of contemporary ceramicists and their unique styles, grouped within twelve themes.

Hugo Morley Fletcher, *Techniques of the World's Greatest Masters of Pottery and Ceramics*. Edison, NJ: Chartwell, 1984. Spotlights various countries in different time periods and their respective styles and methods of pottery making.

Morgen Hall, *The Potter's Primer*. Iola, WI: Krause, 1997. Step-by-step guide to all aspects of creating pottery.

Bernard Leach, *A Potter's Book*. Hollywood, FL: Transatlantic Arts, 1973. Paperback edition, London: Faber & Faber, 1988. First pottery text that dealt with Far Eastern philosophies, styles, and techniques, as well as British slipware. Originally written in 1940.

Charlotte Speight and John Toki, *Hands in Clay: An Introduction to Ceramics*. Columbus, OH: McGraw-Hill, 2003. Comprehensive introductory text about ceramics packed with detailed information and color photographs.

Web Sites

Ceramics Monthly (www.ceramics monthly.org). Published ten times a year, this magazine contains articles and photos on ceramic techniques and styles, as well as detailed profiles of both past and contemporary potters.

Ceramics Today (www.ceramicstoday .com). Interesting and comprehensive site featuring pottery articles and artists from around the world.

Ceramic Studio Prague, Czech Republic (http://ceramic-studio.net/ ceramic-history). Check out the video showing a pot being thrown on the wheel.

Studio Potter (www.studiopotter.org). This professional journal, published in June and December, is for potters, educators, historians, and collectors.

View the work of clay artists at the following Web sites:

Rudy Autio (http://rudyautio.com).

Marek Cecula (http://marekcecula.com/sites/art_works3_foto1.php). (http://marekcecula.com/sites/art_works8_foto2.php).(http://marekcecula.com/sites/art_works9_foto1.php).

Marilyn Levine (http://marilynlevine.com/artworkframeset.html).

Ken Price (http://kenprice.com/category.phleavis.

Paula Winokur (http://paulawinokur.com/currentwork/cw_01.html).

Index

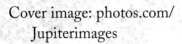

Picture Credits

Cover image: photos.com/
   Jupiterimages

© James L. Amos/Corbis, 21

Art Resource, NY, 30

Bildarchiv Preussischer Kulturbesitz/
   Art Resource, NY, 39

© Christophe Boisvieux/Corbis, 18

© British Museum/Art Resource, NY,
   38, 43, 45, 49, 62, 65

Courtesy of Paula Winokur, 92

© Kevin Fleming/Corbis, 23

Werner Forman/Art Resource, NY,
   33, 51, 67

Giraudon/Art Resource, NY, 9

Hulton Archive/Getty Images, 85

Image copyright © The Metropolitan
   Museum of Art/Art Resource,
   NY, 35, 76

Erich Lessing/Art Resource, NY, 11,
   22, 48, 90

© Craig Lovell/Corbis, 89

Mingei International Museum/Art
   Resource, NY, 78

Réunion des Musées Nationaux/Art
   Resource, NY, 26

© Sakamoto Photo Research
   Laboratory/Corbis, 25

Smithsonian American Art Museum,
   Washington, DC/Art Resource,
   NY, 80, 97

Peter Stackpole/Time Life Pictures/
   Getty Images, 54

© Sandro Vannini/Corbis, 20

Vase, Rookwood Pottery, 1896 by
   Artus van Briggle/Museum of Fine
   Arts, Houston/Gift of Marian
   Thompson Deininger/Bridgeman
   Art Library, 71

Victoria & Albert Museum, London/
   Art Resource, NY, 42, 57, 74, 82

Yale University Art Gallery/Art
   Resource, NY, 70

About the Author

Phyllis Raybin Emert is the author of forty-seven books on a wide variety of subjects—from animals and automobiles to unsolved mysteries and women in the Civil War. This is her second title for Lucent Books. Her first was *Art in Glass*. Phyllis lives in northern New Jersey with her husband Larry and has two grown children and two large dogs.